SPIRITUAL DESERTION

Classics of Reformed Spirituality

This series offers fresh translations of key writings from the seventeenth and eighteenth centuries, making them accessible to the twenty-first-century church. These writings from the "Further Reformation" in the Netherlands offer a balance of doctrine and piety, a mingling of theology and life that has seldom been equaled in the history of Christianity. Each book in this series will provide invaluable insight into a vibrant part of the Christian heritage.

The initial titles to be released are:

- Jean Taffin, *The Marks of God's Children,* 1586
- Jacobus Koelman, *The Duties of Parents,* 1679
- Gisbertus Voetius and Johannes Hoornbeeck, *Spiritual Desertion,* 1659
- Willem Teellinck, *The Path of True Godliness,* 1636

Additional titles are under consideration.

SPIRITUAL DESERTION

Gisbertus Voetius
and Johannes Hoornbeeck

Translated by John Vriend
and Harry Boonstra
Edited by M. Eugene Osterhaven

Baker Academic
A Division of Baker Book House Co
Grand Rapids, Michigan 49516

Published by Baker Academic
a division of Baker Book House Company
P.O. Box 6287, Grand Rapids, MI 49516-6287
www.bakeracademic.com

Printed in the United States of America

Library of Congress Cataloging-in-Publication Data
Voet, Gijsbert, 1589–1676.
[Geestelijke verlatingen. English]
Spiritual desertion / Gisbertus Voetius and Johannes Hoornbeeck ; translated by John Vriend and Harry Boonstra ; edited by M. Eugene Osterhaven.
p. cm.—(Classics of Reformed spirituality)
Includes bibliographical references.
ISBN 0-8010-2646-6 (pbk.)
1. Hidden God. 2. Spiritual life—Reformed Church. I. Hoornbeeck, Johannes. II. Osterhaven, M. Eugene (Maurice Eugene), 1915– III. Title. IV. Series.
BT180.H54V6413 2003
248.4′842—dc21 2003043658

Scripture quotations were translated from the Dutch.

Contents

Series Preface

The *Nadere Reformatie* (a term translated into English as either the "Dutch Second Reformation" or the "Further Reformation") paralleled the historical and spiritual development of English Puritanism in the seventeenth and eighteenth centuries. From its teachers came the watchword of post-Reformation piety: *Ecclesia reformata semper reformanda* ("The church always being reformed").

Proponents of the *Nadere Reformatie* used that phrase to indicate their commitment to the doctrinal and ecclesiological reforms of the Reformation of the sixteenth century as well as to the ongoing reformation of the church. Their intent was not to alter Reformed doctrine. Rather, they proposed the development of a life of piety based on that doctrine within Reformed churches that, in turn, would impact all spheres of life.

Dutch scholars responsible for a periodical on the *Nadere Reformatie* recently formulated the following definition of the movement:

> The Dutch Second (or "Further") Reformation is that movement within the Dutch Reformed Church during the seventeenth and eighteenth centuries, which, as a reaction to the declension or absence of a living faith, made both the personal experience of faith and godliness matters of central importance. From that perspective the movement formulated substantial and procedural reformation initiatives, submitting them to the proper ecclesiastical, political,

> and social agencies, and pursued those initiatives through a further reformation of the church, society, and state in both word and deed.[1]

To further their program of active personal, spiritual, ecclesiastical, and social reformation, the writers of the *Nadere Reformatie* produced some of the finest, most profound literature in the Protestant tradition. Furthermore, because the Dutch Reformed piety of the seventeenth century grew out of Reformed orthodoxy and included among its founders and exponents several erudite orthodox theologians—such as Gisbertus Voetius, Petrus van Mastricht, and Johannes Hoornbeeck—the works of the *Nadere Reformatie* do not give evidence of the kind of antagonism between theology and piety that belonged to the Pietist phase of German Lutheranism. Rather, the proponents of the *Nadere Reformatie* offered a balance of doctrine and piety as well as theology and life that has seldom been equaled in church history.

The *Nadere Reformatie* has generally been overlooked in English-speaking circles due to the lack of primary sources in English. The works of Jean Taffin and Willem Teellinck, two early *Nadere Reformatie* authors, were translated into English in the late sixteenth and early seventeenth centuries, but those now-antiquated translations have not reappeared in more recent times. Moreover, the larger body of works of famous dogmaticians such as Voetius and Hoornbeeck or of pastors such as Theodorus à Brakel, Jacobus Koelman, Jodocus van Lodenstein, Wilhelmus Schortinghuis, and Godefridus Udemans remained untranslated until now. Two exceptions are Alexander Comrie's *ABC of Faith,* first published in English in 1978, and Wilhelmus à Brakel's *Christian's Reasonable Service,* translated into English and published in four volumes in 1992–1995.

The present series addresses the need for further translation of these "old writers," as they are affectionately called by those who know them in Dutch. It also contributes significant biblical and historical insights to the contemporary emphasis on discipleship and spirituality.

In this series, the editors and translators present a representative sampling of the writings of this vibrant movement, along with introductions that open both the texts and the lives of the various authors to the modern reader. The series is intended for the lay reader as

1. *Documentatieblad Nadere Reformatie* 19 (1995): 108.

well as for pastors and scholars, all of whom should benefit from this introduction to the literature of the *Nadere Reformatie* movement, much as the Dutch have benefited from the translation of numerous English Puritan works into their language.

On behalf of the Dutch Reformed Translation Society,
Joel Beeke
James A. De Jong
Richard Muller
Eugene Osterhaven

Introduction

Christians confess that Jesus Christ is Lord and Savior, and they try to honor him in daily life. The fact that they often fail to honor him shows that they share a common sinful humanity and are in need of God's grace.

The "Second Reformation" *(Nadere Reformatie)* in the Netherlands was an attempt to make the daily living of Christians conform to their profession of faith. Similar to Puritanism and other movements dedicated to the deepening of spiritual life in post-Reformation Europe, it greatly influenced the Reformed Church at home and abroad.

A confession of faith and an attempt to express that faith in daily life do not grant Christians immunity from temptation, illness, disappointment, sin, or other problems that plague the fallen human race. All of us are subject to them and respond in some fashion when they strike. Because Christians believe that history, including their own, is under God's control, they see their difficulties in relation to him. They are Christian believers, but they are believers with a burden who are wondering, asking questions of God, and feeling that, at least for the present, he may be abandoning them.

This phenomenon has been a common experience of God's people throughout the ages, as Scripture makes clear. The Psalms are the best example, but the Book of Job, the prophets—think of Jeremiah, for one—and the New Testament offer numerous others. The psalmist cries "out of the depths" to God for help. "To you I call, O Lord my rock; do not refuse to hear me, for if you are silent to me, I will be like those who go down to the pit" (28:1). "I waited patiently for the Lord; he inclined to me and heard my cry. He drew me up from the desolate pit" (40:1–2). The psalmist thirsts for God; his tears have been his food day and night while people have taunted him (42:3); he pleads that God will save him from deep waters and mire (69:2). Although God had been with his people, now they feel that he has rejected them (74:1–2). The psalmist cries out to God because he is "desperate" (88:15); he asks God why he has forsaken him (22:1), words used by the Lord Jesus in his cry of dereliction from the cross.

Fear of desertion, or abandonment, by God was a common experience in the church of the late Middle Ages, and Martin Luther struggled with spiritual depression. A century later, after the successful establishment of reform in a large part of the church in Europe, a "heaviness of heart" became the complaint of many otherwise healthy, pious church people. The Netherlands was no exception, and a number of authors there wrote on the subject.

The seventeenth century was a particularly eventful period in the Netherlands. It was a time of invention and discovery, of prosperity and war, of the triumph of orthodoxy and of pride. Yet there were many in the church who knew the dangers of success and the frailty of even mature Christians. Some of these latter people, who took their religion seriously, were aware of the gulf between profession and practice in themselves and others. Although they believed in the doctrines of sovereign grace, election, and perseverance, they were troubled by doubt and uncertainty that they were children of God. Especially in times of war, pestilence and illness, natural disasters, or other afflictions, they wondered whether God had forgotten or turned his back on them. Aware of the stern warnings given to Israel in the Old Testament and the reality of divine judgment, they needed to be reminded of the promises and faithfulness of God. The fact that those least likely to fall away felt the burden of doubt and abandonment the most is not surprising, for they were the spiritually sensitive folk who wanted to honor their Lord with lives of grateful obedience. It was to such people that many authors with a pastoral heart wrote to comfort and console, demonstrating from Scripture that the concern, or anxiety, of doubting believers was proof that God had not abandoned them; rather, it was evidence of the work of the Spirit in their hearts. Gisbertus

Voetius and Johannes Hoornbeeck, pastors and professors of theology, were among those who gave this subject their attention.

Gisbertus Voetius was born in 1589 to a Dutch family deeply committed to the Reformed faith. Both his father and grandfather died in the struggle against Spain for that faith and the freedom to

The tower (Domtoren) of the cathedral at Utrecht. Photo taken by Brian J. Lee. Used by permission.

Frontispiece of a Dutch publication on the sufferings of the Hungarian ministers sent to the galleys. Among the theological students of Voetius and Hoornbeeck were scores of Hungarians who pondered the possibility of their kin and country being abandoned by God. Muslim Turks had occupied Hungary since 1526. Their cruelty and exploitation of the people shocked all of Europe. However, Jesuits and Hapsburg rulers, in the service of Rome, were the cause of even greater suffering. Whereas 95 percent of the population had embraced Protestantism by 1600, a century later the number had been reduced to roughly 25 percent.

practice it. Voetius inherited their spirit and, with his unusual gifts, made an enormous impression within and beyond his church and country. He began theological studies at Leiden at the age of fifteen. He was there (1604–11) during the early years of the Arminian controversy and accepted the orthodox Reformed positions on sin, grace, free will, and predestination. Later, while pastor of the Reformed Church in Heusden, the town of his birth, he distinguished himself as a delegate to the Synod of Dort (1618–19), which

Facing page: The liberation of Hungarian ministers at Naples by Admiral de Ruyter, 1676. The men pictured had been sold to a Spanish fleet to serve as galley slaves. Chained to oars day and night for nine months, some had struggled with the fear of abandonment by God as well as their fellow believers. The twenty-six survivors sang Psalms 46, 114, and 125 as they were being transferred to a Dutch ship on February 11, 1676. When the transfer was complete, they knelt on deck in their rags and emaciated condition and sang Psalm 116. The Dutch seamen, who seldom shed tears, wept openly.

condemned Arminianism. Thereafter, Voetius served his regional synod on various commissions and so impressed his peers with his pastoral work, scholarship, and writings that in 1634 he was called to teach theology and oriental languages at a newly established school in Utrecht that would later become a university. Within two years he became its head, and under him the school achieved an international reputation and attracted foreign students. Some came from as far away as Hungary, the first of these arriving in 1643. They were so impressed by the learning and Calvinistic theological stance of Voetius and by the type of sincere Reformed peity that they experienced in the lecture hall, dining hall, and pulpit that they sent the message to their schools back home. As a result, more young men made the long journey to Utrecht—a thousand miles for some—to observe and study. Some years over one-half of the student body was from Hungary.

What they heard was standard Reformed theology presented in a scholastic manner with logical analysis, precise definition, careful organization, and an examination of opposing views. Voetius had learned this method from medieval and Reformed theologians who had preceded him. Of the latter, especially John Calvin and Franciscus Gomarus, his own professor at Leiden, were important in his development. The content of his theology was similar to that of the Reformed theologians whose writings he knew. Thus, it was unlike that of the medieval masters who relied too heavily on unaided human reason and neglected Scripture, according to Voetius. But students did not hear lectures merely on doctrine derived from Scripture. To be faithful to revelation, Voetius taught, theology had to be practical and lead to a lifestyle that glorifies God. The "practice of piety" *(praxis pietatis; de praktijk der godzaligheid)* lay at the heart of his work as a theologian and pastor, and it is the title of a work in which he describes in detail what it means to live—and to die—as a Christian.

A striking feature of Voetius's work was his examination and criticism of what he considered to be false teachings in the theological world of his day. Among these were the errors of Roman Catholicism and Arminianism, and he exposed them in lectures and writings throughout his career. Since the teachings of Rome are well known, comment about them here is unnecessary. A brief description of Arminianism, however, may be helpful.

Jacobus Arminius (1560–1609) had been one of Voetius's teachers at Leiden. Voetius, therefore, witnessed the development of his ideas with unusual interest. As a student in Geneva, Arminius had reacted against the strong predestinarianism of his teacher, Theodore Beza, and at Leiden had encountered a similar stance in his colleague Gomarus. Rejecting the doctrine of unconditional election, Arminius held that election depends on the human response. God has foreknowledge of that response but does not determine it. The human will is not fallen but remains free; we can believe or resist grace. Christ died for all, but faith is necessary for salvation. Arminius's teaching was not new in the church; it was reminiscent of Pelagianism and Semi-Pelagianism, which had been condemned in church councils centuries earlier. When some people holding Arminius's positions embraced Socianism, with its denial of Christ, Voetius attacked Arminianism with added fervor.

The philosophy of René Descartes (1596–1650), who moved to the Netherlands in 1629 and wrote his most important works there, won an audience with his appeal to common sense and human reason. Descartes came under fire because Voetius thought his exaltation of human reason denigrated faith, the need for Scripture, and the illumination of the Holy Spirit.

In his polemical activity, Voetius also opposed the teaching of a popular theologian who taught at both Franeker and Leiden. Johannes Cocceius (1603–69) desired a biblical theology that did justice to the strong emphasis in Scripture on history and God's covenantal relations with humankind. Fearful of speculation and reacting to some of the Calvinist spirit of his times, Cocceius held that Scripture made the history of salvation rather than God's eternal decree the controlling concept in the interpretation of revelation. Covenant, he said, is "nothing other than a divine declaration of the method of perceiving the love of God and of obtaining union and communion with him." The covenants were initiated by God, but they required a human response. The various covenants made with God's people in history lead to a final consummation promised in Scripture. Thus, Cocceius's covenantal theology had a strong eschatological character and won a wide following. Voetius, however, felt that Cocceius's heavy emphasis on history compromised the doctrine of God's eternal decree and sovereignty over history. Moreover, Voetius held that Cocceius exaggerated the importance

René Descartes
(1596–1650)

of the character of the diverse periods within history and erred in teaching that, inasmuch as the Sabbath was a part of the ceremonial law for God's people in an earlier dispensation, it was not binding under the new covenant of grace. Cocceius's covenant theology weathered the storm of Voetius's criticism, and subsequent Reformed theology adopted many of its emphases while maintaining the traditional teaching of God's eternal decree.

Another school of thought that arose within the church during Voetius's years of service and against which he felt called to contend was Labadism. It was named after its founder, Jean de Labadie (1610–74), a former Jesuit who embraced the Reformed faith in 1650 and brought with him extreme pietistic ideas. A gifted leader, he was characterized by one observer who went to Geneva to witness personally a remarkable revival going on there under Labadie's leadership as "an Ambrose in heart and apostolic respectability, a Chrysostom in eloquence, an Augustine in love, [and] a Bernard in salving fervor." Labadie preached in various places on the Continent, including the Netherlands, and attracted followers who had similar interests in reforming the church. An eleven-day stop in Utrecht brought him into contact with Voetius. With little appreciation for the church as an institution and strong criticism of the Dutch Reformed Church, which he felt needed "radical surgery" and whose pastors needed "conversion," he gathered those considered truly pious into small groups of "born again believers" for "prophetic exercises." Their worship was simple, devoid of any formal, liturgical prayer. Scripture was said to be understood only by the immediate inspiration of the Holy Spirit, and the sacraments were rarely celebrated. The community shared goods, and marriage to a person considered to be unregenerate was nonbinding. The children of couples within the inner circle belonged to the Lord. While appreciating their earnest spirit, Voetius believed that the Labadists' rejection of the institutional church, with its offices, sacraments, and formal worship, was wrong and that some of their other beliefs and practices were dangerous if not unbiblical. He disliked their sectarian, independent spirit and sought to correct their errors, but the movement survived and its spirit lingered long in the church.

Johannes Cocceius (1603–69)

Jean de Labadie (1610–74)

Not the least of Voetius's concerns was freedom of the church to govern itself, a problem that seems unreal to us today but that was serious at the time. Thomas Erastus, a Swiss theologian who had been appointed professor of medicine at Heidelberg in 1558, held that the state had authority over church organization, belief, and practice. The relation of the church to civil authorities had been discussed before in the Netherlands; the States General had called the Synod of Dort and had sent to it eighteen of its own delegates. Erastianism, as this theory of state control of the church was called, had also been evident at the Westminster Assembly (1643–49), which had been called by the civil government in England.

Much of the polemical activity mentioned above took place in meetings organized by Voetius on Saturdays. Issues facing the church were presented, students were appointed to argue for and against them, and 358 of the debates were summarized and published by Voetius in five volumes.

Lest it appear that polemics was Voetius's main activity, we note that he lectured regularly on theological subjects; that he spent countless hours in his study; that he and his wife of sixty-four years had ten children, two of whom followed their father as professors at Utrecht; that his pastoral heart moved him to catechize orphans and call on many sick folk; and that he was a prolific writer and member of the "Utrecht Circle."

The Utrecht Circle, often called the "Voetian Circle" *(De Voetsiaanse Kring)* because many of its participants had been his students, was a fellowship of "kindred spirits" that met regularly in the home of the distinguished Van Schurman family, whose two remaining members, both unmarried, were Anna Marie and Johan Godschalk Van Schurman. It was Johan, a physician, who had visited Labadie in Geneva and had brought back the favorable report, and it was his sister, Anna Marie, one of the most famous women in Dutch history, who was hostess to this unusual group of scholars, pastors, and other leaders committed to a Second Reformation within the Dutch Reformed Church. Anna Marie was instrumental in getting Labadie to the Netherlands, and when he left the Reformed Church, she joined a conventicle that he organized in Rotterdam. Her departure and the death of other members of the Utrecht Circle were disheartening to Voetius, but Jodocus van Lodenstein, pastor of the Domkerk in

Anna Marie Van Schurman (1607–78)

Utrecht, began hosting meetings of the group, and Voetius continued his extraordinary labors until his death on November 1, 1676.

Gisbertus Voetius was called a "Rock of Gibraltar" by his colleagues and friends. Critics referred to him as "the pope of Utrecht" *(de paus van Utrecht).* His influence there was indeed great. Its school was often referred to as the Voetian Academy *(Academia Voetiana).* At his funeral, after his forty-two years in Utrecht, he was called "a giant among trail blazers." A eulogy quoted by Joel Beeke in his study of Voetius is apropos: "Few men have in any age exercised greater influence over the church of their time and country."[1]

The sheer volume of Voetius's publications is impressive, and he usually completed what he began. An exception is the present work, a subject much discussed in his time. After he began writing on "spiritual abandonments," he turned the work over to one of his former students who had become a colleague on the Utrecht faculty. Johannes Hoornbeeck (1617–66), a child prodigy who took up the study of Latin at the age of six, began his theological studies at Leiden but transferred to the University of Utrecht so he could sit at the feet of Voetius. After a few years in parish ministry, he became a professor and pastor in Utrecht, where he worked alongside Voetius and became a member of the Utrecht Circle. As expected, Hoornbeeck became a learned, influential Reformed theologian with emphases similar to those of his respected teacher and mentor. He also became an influential polemicist, writing a three-volume work against Socinianism and treatises on other traditions within the church and non-Christian religions.

In 1654, Hoornbeeck became professor of theology at the University of Leiden, where he continued to serve the interests of the Second Reformation. He had a passion for missions throughout his career, and at Leiden he published a work on that subject. Another of his studies on missions appeared after his death. His writings on theology and ethics followed the lines of Voetius's thought, and he won high acclaim as an orthodox theologian who lived what he professed to believe. Because of his ability and popularity, Hoornbeeck was often invited to preach, and, like Voetius, he assumed other pastoral work as well. Also like Voetius, he was admired by his students and colleagues as an indefatigable worker. He may have worked too

1. Joel Beeke, *Gisbertus Voetius* (Grand Rapids: Reformation Heritage Books, 1999), 36.

hard, as friends feared, for he aged prematurely and died before he was fifty years old.

Because they believed that true theology should be practical, that faith should result in disciplined, holy living, Voetius, Hoornbeeck, and their friends were considered "precisionists" *(preciesen)* or "earnest ones" *(de ernstigen)* by their contemporaries. Detractors called them "sanctimonians" *(de fijnen),* but the fact is they brought new life into the church, and through the church they were a blessing to their nation and beyond.

The first edition of *Spiritual Desertion (Geestelijke Verlatingen)* appeared in 1646, and an improved edition was published in 1659. It was republished in modern Dutch by the Gereformeerd Traktaatgenotschap *Filippus* (The Reformed Tract Society *Filippus*) in 1898. It was written because of the biblical admonition to rejoice in the Lord and to live victoriously as his children, whereas many fellow Christians manifested a lack of delight in God and were filled with fears and anxieties. The noble intention of Voetius and Hoornbeeck is as relevant today as it was in the seventeenth century. The breakdown of morality, environmental problems, terrorism, and, of course, the perpetual problem of indwelling sin, not to mention other concerns, are certain to generate feelings of spiritual abandonment. The message of Voetius and Hoornbeeck is needed today.

M. Eugene Osterhaven

Gisbertus Voetius (1589–1676)

Spiritual Desertion

by Gisbertus Voetius

In the practice and pursuit of godliness, the Christian struggle is by no means the most minor part. In this struggle, we must consider and observe:

- Christian warriors and their weapons
- the enemies that oppose them
- the struggle or combat itself and the ways in which the enemies are opposed
- the resistance offered

The enemies are all sorts of difficulties in this life, both those that are shameful and those that make one sad. The shameful are all sorts of mistakes and sins, with their allurements and stimuli; the sad ones are all sorts of sorrows and trials, which in turn are spiritual (or internal) and physical (or external). External sorrows are illness, poverty, persecution, and so forth. Internal sorrows are spiritual abandonments and temptations.

In this volume, we will skip over other enemies and parts of the struggle and will deal with and explain only spiritual desertion, or abandonment. We will successively discuss:

1. the nature and characteristics of spiritual desertion
2. the remedies or antitoxins against them and the method or manner of their healing
3. certain questions or cases of conscience to which we hope to respond

Distinction of Terms

In order to keep words from being ambiguous, we wish first of all to warn the reader that the practical writers[1] often confuse and equate in their writings the following matters: temptation or the struggle between the flesh and the spirit; a sick and disturbed conscience; abandonment or the struggle of one's conscience; struggle and temptation by Satan; a heartless practice of religion; mental or spiritual grief; a sense of the wrath of God and the struggle with it; desolation or despondency; spiritual lack or dryness. The point of view from which and the words and terms with which all these matters are expressed must nevertheless be carefully distinguished in order to save the authors in question from, or deliver them from, real or seeming contradiction. The words *temptation* and *abandonment,* or *desertion,* are used most frequently here and must therefore be defined correctly.

Temptation is either human, diabolical, or divine.

1. Human temptation is either good or evil. Good is the kind of testing by which people examine others or themselves as it concerns the ordinary or also the supernatural gifts and goods. "Examine yourselves whether you are in the faith" (2 Cor. 13:5). "Let a person examine himself or herself and so eat of the bread and drink of the cup" (1 Cor. 11:28). But it is evil when in practicing it a person tempts God, others, or oneself. "Let no one say when he is tempted, 'I am tempted by God.' For God cannot be tempted with evil, and he himself tempts no one. But each person is tempted when he is lured and enticed by his own desire" (James 1:13–14).

2. Diabolical temptation occurs when the devil (especially called the tempter, Matt. 4:3) opposes people, either externally with his agitations and torments or internally with his evil promptings, to bring them to unbelief, despair, disobedience, and all kinds of sins. On this subject a great deal has been written by interpreters of and practical writers on Matthew 4, 2 Corinthians 12, and Ephesians 6.

3. Divine "temptation" is the testing by which God wisely and justly tests a person. He does this either by commanding that person to perform a certain deed, as in the case of Abraham: "And after

1. Dutch: *practizijns.* The reference is to the authors who write about the practice of godliness, especially those of the Second Reformation. Voetius and Hoornbeeck often quote from these authors without providing documentation.

these things God tested Abraham and said to him, 'Abraham!' And he said, 'Behold, here am I.' And he said, 'Now take your son, your only son whom you love, Isaac, and go to the land of Moriah, and offer him there as a burnt offering upon one of the mountains of which I shall tell you" (Gen. 22:1–2), or by permitting and directing the temptations of the devil, the world, and the flesh. "You shall not listen to the words of that prophet or to that dreamer of dreams; for the Lord your God is testing you to know whether you love the Lord your God with all your heart and with all your soul" (Deut. 13:3). "God is faithful, and he will not let you be tempted beyond your strength, but with the temptation will also provide the way of escape, that you may be able to endure it" (1 Cor. 10:13). "And to keep me from being too elated by the perfection of the revelations, a thorn was given me in the flesh, a messenger of Satan, to harass me that I might not be too elated. Three times I besought the Lord about this, that he should leave me alone. But he said to me, 'My grace is sufficient for you, for my power is made perfect in weakness'" (2 Cor. 12:7–9). See also 2 Samuel 24:1 compared to 1 Chronicles 21:1. God also tempts (tests) us by withdrawing from us the sense of his consoling grace and fatherly favor. This is especially called spiritual abandonment, the kind of spiritual abandonment we now intend to treat in particular.

Divine Desertion

Divine desertion is differentiated in terms of whether it occurs in relation to the wicked or in relation to the elect.

In relation to the wicked, it is either particular and special by giving them up to a specific sin, temptation, or trial: "And the Spirit of the Lord departed from Saul, and an evil spirit from the Lord tormented him" (1 Sam. 16:14; also see 1 Sam. 28:15), or universal (general), complete, and entire, insofar as the Lord abandons them to themselves and never lets them come to the enjoyment of his grace and glory.

In relation to the elect, divine abandonment occurs either before or after the calling and the actual conversion.

Before conversion he abandons them as it concerns the inflow of his grace and actual communication and communion with them so that abandonment on the part of the abandoned, and as far as they are concerned, is complete. However, on God's part, and as far as he is concerned, it is almost complete, except for a thin and intangible little thread, an influx or rather an afflux and (so to speak) circumambient flux or near flux by which he saves and keeps them for himself.

The desertion of the elect after the calling (which at that point is not decisive or in any way complete) consists of sin, temptation, an external cross and trial, disconsolateness, abandonment to solitariness, or inner insensitivity.

Desertion in sin occurs when God refrains from granting his own the second grace, namely, to arouse and lead them, and that to their humiliation, as in the case of Peter's fall, of which Augustine speaks as follows: "I make bold to say that it is useful for the proud to fall into a public and well-known sin and so become dissatisfied with themselves, inasmuch as by pleasing themselves they had already fallen. For Peter was in a healthier condition when he wept and was dissatisfied with himself than when he boldly put himself first and satisfied himself."

Desertion in temptation, or testing, occurs when God prevents victory over it but does not remove it (see 2 Cor. 12:8–9 cited above).

Desertion in terms of an external cross occurs when God does not come to our aid with his present assistance. "For the Lord has called you like a wife forsaken and grieved in spirit, nevertheless, you are the wife of youth although you have been forsaken, says your God. For a brief moment I have forsaken you, but with great compassion I will gather you" (Isa. 54:6–7; see also Isa. 60:15; 62:4).

Desertion in disconsolateness and spiritual numbness occurs when the Lord God refrains from blessing his elect with a feeling of the sweetness of consoling grace.

This is the desertion we will now consider in somewhat greater detail. It can be called "temptation" [testing] on the part of God, who examines the faith and love of his own, although the term is also used with reference to the diabolical attacks that frequently accompany or follow this abandonment by God. It may also be called coldness of heart, distraction of the mind and spirit, and darkening of one's consciousness, because all these things result from it. In addition, it is called assault, combat, struggle, and that by virtue of its consequence, because on the occasion of this desertion we have to struggle with the devil, with our own flesh, with the evil assaults of people's mistaken opinions (as Job had to with his friends). It is also called the contention and agitation of conscience, and further, spiritual depression and despondency, since these mental states necessarily flow from this desertion. Some practical writers call it spiritual disconsolateness, dryness, insensibility, deficiency. Sometimes it is used very broadly so that it includes not only the suffering and this mental illness itself but also its circumstances and consequences. At other times, people use it in a more restricted sense so that it refers solely and specifically to the desertion itself.

By itself and in terms of its nature, such desertion is not a sin but a gift of God's grace, in the way of withholding and not of adding (as it is called). "For it has been granted to you that for the sake of Christ you should not only believe in him but also suffer for his sake, being engaged in the same conflict which you saw and now hear to be mine," that is, a cross and fatherly chastisement (Phil. 1:29–30).

Definition of Spiritual Desertion

We describe spiritual desertion as follows: It is an inner cross or spiritual sorrow and trial as a result of which a person, now being truly converted to God, fails to feel his or her heart's delight in God and divine things. It results from the darkening of one's assurance and clarity with respect to appropriation by a personal faith. The worst but least frequent occurrence is the suffering of a constant painful deficiency; a more frequent occurrence is the cross of believers; most frequent is the inner cross.

The mental states, the good condition and configuration, gift, or grace that are opposed to this lack or deficiency are spiritual peace, consolation, sweetness, and enjoyment, first of all in our God, further in divine things, that is, the elements, workings, means, and instruments of saving grace. But this constant lack touched upon a moment ago is only for a time, not forever, or to the very end. "For a brief moment I forsook you" (Isa. 54:7). "For his anger is but for a moment, but his favor is for a lifetime. Weeping may tarry for the night, but joy comes with the morning" (Ps. 30:5). This suffering is partial, not total. In fact, it is a temporary cessation and lack of joy and serenity, not so much as it concerns the root but the fruit, not so much as it relates to the presence and essence but rather to the feeling and the exercise. "So then," says Christ, "you have sorrow now, but I will see you again and your hearts will rejoice, and no one will take your joy from you" (John 16:22). "And the ransomed of the LORD will return and come to Zion with singing; everlasting joy will be upon their heads; they will obtain joy and gladness, and sorrow and sighing will flee away. . . . Yours shall be everlasting joy" (Isa. 51:11; 61:7; cf. Gal. 5:22). "Rejoice in the Lord always; again I will say, Rejoice" (Phil. 4:4). "In this you rejoice, though now for a little while you may have to suffer various trials" (1 Peter 1:6).

The lessening and removal of joy and spiritual enjoyment occur with regard to its object (that is, the thing for which it is active) in two ways. It occurs either with regard to God our Father, of whom it is therefore said that he averts and hides his face. "Why do you hide your face and count me as your enemy?" (Job 13:24). "When you hid your face, I was dismayed" (Ps. 30:7). It also occurs with respect to the grace of God or to the means of grace and the exercises of godliness when delight and sweetness in reading, listening to, and meditating on God's Word, in the commandments, and in the use of the sacraments are no longer felt. This is why this abandonment is regularly called by a special name: spiritual dryness and unfeeling practice, a subject often mentioned in the works of Roman Catholic writers. We may well adopt, be it with mature judgment, some of the points made by these Roman authors. See, among others, Jan van Ruysbroeck and Thomas à Kempis in his *Imitation of Christ,* and so forth. We must, however, as stated, exercise caution here, since the authors referred to—in accordance with their theological presuppositions—wrap up and confuse these matters with the possibility of the cessation of faith and with doubt and uncertainty concerning the possible discontinuation of grace so that they do not rightly understand or at least lack the courage to confess the causes of this disease and the manner of healing it.

The true subjects of this desertion, the people in whose life it is found, are only believers, for this is *their* peculiar and incommunicable kind of suffering and illness, just as eclipses only occur in the case of the sun and the moon. Unbelievers and hypocrites are only "wandering stars" (Jude 13), not those two great lights. Hence in them that which was never there cannot be eclipsed and lacking. The more precisely defined subject, and the injured part in the believer, formally speaking, is really the will—as it pertains to the base, i.e., the intellect, and that in the faculty we call conscience, the faculty by which human beings reflect on, bear knowledge of, make judgments about their state, and perceptibly appropriate for themselves the grace of God in particular. This is why these abandonments are referred to by the name conscience, which is their underlying subject.

From this it follows that those who do not correctly grasp and understand the nature of these abandonments think that the essence or peculiar nature of abandonment consists of mental distractions and digressions, which however are the antecedent cause; or in some injury and weakening of the conscience, which in fact is really a proof of the continuation of the illness; or desperation, accompanied by the wrath of God or, at least, what the subjects think is the wrath of God, in the struggle with despair, in spiritual dread or sadness, in diabolical promptings and temptations, all of which are really the visible signs and consequences of this illness; or in the temptation of the flesh to sin and some permission or sheltering of this tendency. Usually all these things precede the abandonment, but sometimes they accompany and follow it.

Causes of Spiritual Desertion

Now follow the operative causes. The first is God, who in his fatherly way sends and governs the abandonments. He does not send them, however, by any active operation but by a deficient or (so to speak) negative effect, called withdrawal by others, when he does not palpably pour out his love in the hearts of believers and does not visit them with the taste of his loveliness, as we learn from Romans 5:5: "And hope does not put us to shame because God's love has been poured into our hearts through the Holy Spirit which has been given to us." "And I will pray the Father and he will give . . ." [and so forth] (John 14:16–18). "Without having seen him you love him; though you do not now see him, you believe in him and rejoice with unutterable and exalted joy" (1 Peter 1:8). "You have tasted that the Lord is good" (1 Peter 2:3).

The second cause, the principal and most immediate and operative cause, is the lack of a clear appropriation by faith. That is to say, when the certainty of a clear and distinct faith and the palpable enjoyment of it ceases, so does the joy and jubilation of the heart.

When the spiritual eating and drinking stops, so also and immediately does the spiritual intoxication. "I have come into my garden, my sister, my bride. I have gathered my myrrh with my spice. I have eaten my honeycomb with my honey. I have drunk my wine along with my milk. Eat, O friends, and drink. Drink deeply, O lovers! . . . I opened to my beloved, but my beloved had turned and gone. My soul failed me when he spoke. I sought him but found him not. I called him but he gave no answer" (Song of Sol. 5:1, 6).

The internal and motivating causes can be diverse, such as ignorance and a lack of skill in spiritual matters; a presumptuous, doubting, or timid conscience; an incautious, untimely, and overly inquisitive consideration of the doctrine of election, reprobation, hardening, the sin against the Holy Spirit, the sovereignty of God, the severity of his judgment, and so forth. Belonging here as well are the fall into a grave sin or entertaining a hidden sin; excessive permissiveness and inattention as a result of which believers may doze on the pillows of daily sins of weakness, lukewarmness, and laxness in the exercises of godliness and in the proper observance and custody of one's heart and ways; mental preoccupation and distraction in prayer and meditation; a false freedom of heart and mind, spiritual gluttony and satedness; presumption, carelessness, and complacency with respect to heavenly consolations; carelessness with respect to the well-being of both the natural and supernatural dimensions of life coupled with a lessening of spiritual poverty or deficiency and of the desire to move out of this tent. "For while we are still in this tent we sigh, being burdened; not that we would be unclothed but that we would be further clothed, so that what is mortal may be swallowed up by life" (2 Cor. 5:4). "Wretched human being that I am! Who will deliver me from this body of death?" (Rom. 7:24).

Add to this the stirrings and danger of vainglory and spiritual pride (see Ps. 30:7 and 2 Cor. 12:7, words already cited earlier); finally also the censure of and resistance to our conscience when it witnesses against sins, accompanied by a spiritual narrowness that often so increases that people begin to think that they lack both the gifts of grace, which they do possess, as well as those they do not.

External causes and occasions are: a cross, and all sorts of external burdens; reading, hearing but not rightly discerning and appropriating the things in Scripture that are most conducive to a rigorous examination of one's conscience and to the removal of hypocrisy or pretense. Also to be mentioned here are the observation and incautious appropriation of any grave divine judgment upon the ungodly, hypocrites, indeed, even upon his own children.

Secondary Matters

We divide the secondary matters as follows:

1. the things that accompany or follow desertion
2. some matters that are peculiar to desertion
3. the marks of desertion

1. The things that accompany abandonment or follow this disease are threefold:

(1) those that always accompany desertion
(2) those that almost always accompany desertion
(3) those that sometimes accompany desertion

(1) The things that *always* accompany desertion are the aversion to or non-acceptance of consolation. Listen to David: "In the day of my trouble I sought the Lord; in the night my hand was stretched incessantly; my soul refused to be comforted" (Ps. 77:2). Those who are thus minded tend to regard the consolations too lightly and the consolers suspect, as if they did not sufficiently bear in mind the justice of God and the gravity of sin and badly neglected the mercy of God. And although they sometimes listen to these consolations with some desire and joy, they cannot feel and accept their plainness and reality in such a manner that they can find peace there but continue to be suspended between hope and fear, assent and refusal. One always also finds their pains, anxieties, and a steady maelstrom

of concerns, particularly the fear of falling into sins and being put to shame before their conscience.

A common phenomenon as well is the search for solitude and the concealment of evil, the disclosure and confession of which can hardly be obtained even by intimate friends. One can add to this list all kinds of temptations and spiritual trials, not so much to sin and in relation to that which we have to obey but with respect to the truth and contemplative knowledge of the faith, of conversion, of one's state, and, by implication, of election, calling, justification, and the perseverance of the saints. Actually, we need not especially discuss these temptations (which are essentially distinct from spiritual abandonment) here because we can read and inquire about them in William Ames, *Cases of Conscience;* William Couper, *Anatomy of the Conscience;* Robert Linacker, *Consolation of the Troubled Conscience;* John Abernethy, *A Heavenly Treatise Containing Physicke for Souls;* and, at length, William Perkins in a variety of treatises, and after him John Downame in *Spiritual Conflict,* and finally—very thoroughly and succinctly—Robert Bolton in *Instructions for a Right Comforting of Afflicted Consciences.*

(2) The circumstances that *most frequently* accompany abandonment are the external cross of poverty, disease, adversity, persecutions, and so forth; depression; considerable physical weakness that often results in a slow but certain death. An example of the first is David. "When I declared not my sin, my body wasted away, through my groaning all day long. Day and night your hand was heavy upon me; my strength was dried up as by the heat of summer" (Ps. 32:3–4). "Let the bones which you have broken rejoice" (Ps. 51:8). A second example is Robert Glover, a martyr later in life, with whom we shall deal in greater detail after this. An example of the latter is Francis Spira, whose history is well known. This history ought to be read and can be read, since it is available in more than one language.

(3) The circumstances that *sometimes* accompany or follow this evil are demonic possession in a physical sense; certain horrors and torments that Satan manages to introduce into the soul through the senses and the imagination of waking or sleeping people; diabolical incitements to utter taunts or blasphemies and to commit suicide, a fact also noted by Downame, Abernethy, and, among Roman Catholics, by Bonaventure in his work *On the Growth of Religion;* finally, the struggle with death and martyrdom. Of the

first, Robert Bolton has two examples that we will cite; of the second, we will cite the same Bolton and William Perkins in his *Treatise on Spiritual Abandonments,* from Fox's *Book of Martyrs* in the person of Robert Glover.

2. The matters that are peculiar to divine abandonment and can therefore be called positive are:

(1) The fact that this torment is the worst, far exceeding all external torments. The reason for this can be inferred from Proverbs 18:14: "A person's spirit will endure sickness, but who will lift up a broken spirit?"

(2) The fact that for believers it is, by virtue of commonality and resemblance, like the death of the soul ("for the steadfast love of the Lord is better than life") and like the descent into hell, so to speak, a situation I would rather describe with the words of Henri Harpius than with my own. In his second book, chapter 47, the author speaks as follows: "But this can be called a hellish infirmity in which the soul lies down, not on account of love but on account of anxiety and inner conflict, nowhere finding any comfort, neither in God nor in any creature." And this occurs because, after God had drawn and attracted the soul "so near and so intensely to himself that all the consolations of things that can console us apart from God have become for it a cross and a trial, the Most High now casts it from himself and puts it down naked and bare. Then these believers sit, hungry, between two tables, that is, between spiritual and carnal delights; the soul despises the carnal and the spiritual refuses God." Robert Bolton speaks very movingly about the gravity of this inner conflict in *Instructions for a Right Comforting of Afflicted Consciences.*

(3) The fact that among the friends of God there are few or none who have not at some time, at least for a short while, experienced it.

The properties one could call negative are the following:

(1) The fact that the habitus, that is, the essence and habit of faith, is not removed, indeed, not even diminished.[2]

What this means is that one's faith is definitely not gone as a result of the impact and assaults of temptation when one's conscience fails to feel and taste the sweetness of God's grace and of justification—for which it nevertheless yearns and which it continually pursues with much sighing. On the contrary, faith is like a

2. This is most strikingly treated by John Downame in his *Spiritual Conflict.*

smoldering piece of charcoal covered with ashes (a simile that practical writers tend to employ in this connection). The case is that in this state of numbness faith itself is not so much diminished as concealed and obscured, as concerns its functions, when the black cloud of depression or spiritual abandonment interposes itself between the two. One's faith, in that condition, has retreated into some corner of the heart and stays there, as the practical writers teach with their similes. Faith and assurance are then still found as it pertains to the root, the ground, the state, and the possession of it, as well as to some of the activities that flow from that possession, but not as it pertains to the outflow and influence of the manifestation and assurance, the emotions, the consolation, the joy and serenity, as it was experienced earlier. Similarly, some of the practical writers also make a distinction between the certainty of a clear consciousness (obviousness) and that of "adherence," as Robert Bolton and others do.

Corresponding to this is what William Ames says in *The Marrow,* namely, that as it concerns feeling, this assurance of faith is not always present. For it can happen and often does, either as a consequence of impaired judgment or of various temptations and disturbances of the mind, that the one who truly believes and is justified before God by faith nevertheless thinks for a time—in keeping with what he feels—that he does not truly believe and is not reconciled with God.

This abandonment is still further known by comparisons with the abandonment and temptation of Christ. He neither saw nor tasted the goodness of God in his feelings, as he was accustomed, when he lamented that he was forsaken; nevertheless, he believed and could not but believe that God was his God. The reason for this was that our sins and the wrath of God upon them were interposed between the Father and the Son like a cloud and held back and obstructed the influence of his deity so that his humanity could suffer on our behalf.

This is the source of the pronouncements made by the "old writers": "The suffering of Christ was the sweet sleep of his deity. Christ held back the rays of his deity so that his humanity would suffer." And again: "He did not cancel out the personal union itself but the enjoyment of it." In the same way, the children of God who are full of spiritual knowledge, godliness, and faith tend to be most abandoned so that, though they display the assurance of adherence (when they cling firmly and faithfully to their God), they are nevertheless unable to feel with joy the certainty of the manifestation, though with penitence and tears they seek it with the utmost intensity.

(2) The second mark, then, is that not all the activities of faith cease, for people can still lean on God, cling to him, and desire his grace while being unable, by a reciprocal and self-reflective knowledge of their state, to decide with an evident and sensible certainty in their own favor and obtain comfort from that fact.

(3) The third of these characteristics is that those who suffer this affliction and its accompaniments do not doubt or despair, although they too, being moved for a time by strong feeling and impaired judgment, utter words usually heard only from the mouths of despairing people, as they cry out that they are desperate and fear or mistakenly suspect of themselves that they do not have a grain of faith.

3. The marks by which this ailment is known can be readily inferred by anyone from the causes and characteristics we have now explained. The antecedent phenomena can be known from the purpose and consequences of abandonment that we will now explain. Let it be sufficient for us to point out only a few marks of distinction by which desertion can be distinguished from a melancholic disorder, from despair and demonic possession—a condition with which it is mistakenly confused by the inexperienced.

It is distinguished from melancholia as follows. In the first place, a melancholic disorder is directly lodged in the imagination, but abandonment is located in the rational soul.

Second, the symptoms of melancholia are pain and fear without the kind of discernible cause the depressed could advance to explain them, but the abandoned show by a sharp and refined judgment that they know the cause of their disturbance and the total mystery of the temptations and promptings of Satan and can make sense of them by their answers as well as their excuses, their refutations and replies.

Third, this desertion can exist and is frequently there (as the most competent and experienced practical writers such as Perkins, Downame, Abernethy, and Bolton attest) when a person's temperament and physical condition show no tendency to melancholia and when also no bad humor, intestinal diseases, and such ailments can in any way be found. But this is not true of melancholia.

Fourth, melancholics are most afraid of fantastic and illusory vanities that do not now exist nor have ever existed, as this has been unfolded in the work of the practical writers. Examples are Andrew Lawrence *(On Melancholia)* and such theologians as John Gerson and Perkins *(Cases of Conscience)*. The abandoned, on the other hand, fear only the prospect of becoming insensitive to the grace of God and of coming under his wrath.

Fifth, melancholia is not accompanied by fever, while desertion often is.[3]

Sixth, melancholia is often cured by medical treatment and medicines, but this is by no means true for abandonment.

Seventh, melancholia is often alleviated or eliminated by recreation, physical diversion, and mental entertainment, by games, music, and song, by the speeches and conversations of comical and farcical entertainers, and so forth, but these measures only intensify the bitterness and severity of desertion and its attendant woes.

Finally, melancholics as well as old fogies are incapable of doing certain things, but the abandoned surpass not only others but often even themselves in intellect and memory, wisdom and prudence, respecting divine and human matters.

The abandoned are also distinguished from the despairing or desperate, (1) because the abandoned eagerly look for the Lord and continually look forward to his presence and consolation; (2) because, while they inwardly grieve over the loss of consolation, they are most saddened by their sins and imperfections; (3) because they are not absolutely and totally averse to the exercises of godliness, to say nothing of the idea that they would continually and deliberately break out in blasphemies against God and divine things; (4) because they do not break out in sins and a variety of roguish actions toward God and their neighbors; (5) because by virtue of their own spiritual impulses or because they were admonished to that end by others, they seek the Lord and the means of attaining union with him and frequently sigh to him. This is a sign that they

3. Could the opposite perhaps be intended here, namely, that melancholia is accompanied by fever and abandonment is not? One reason for this question is that immediately following this statement the author refers to external means for the treatment of melancholia but not for the treatment of abandonment.

still cherish some hope and think that there is perhaps still some love and mercy stored up for them in God's fatherly heart, although they themselves can no longer savor the sweetness of it in their own hearts.

The abandoned are further differentiated from those who are physically demon-possessed (1) because the diabolical act of taking possession of and violating people as a rule immediately robs them at the very start of the use of their external senses, of the ability to stand and move freely, but abandonment does not do this; (2) because in the case of the possessed the limbs of the body are often stretched and mutilated, but this too does not happen in the case of the abandoned; (3) because the devil, by means of words, deeds, workings, and other signs, manifests himself, and therefore his craftiness and power and the resulting agitation in the possessed are easily recognized. Granted, some theologians ascribe to believers, found in abandonment or temptation, the condition of desperation or despair, but this diagnosis must be taken and understood with the gift of discernment. For, to tell the truth, they cannot despair but only wrestle with despair, utter words of despair, suspect or mistakenly think, indeed even before bystanders, that they despair and thus in some ways display such symptoms as are also seen in those who are in fact desperate.

Why God Allows Desertion

The immediate ends for which God sends desertion, or abandonment, are: that the believer may be tested and so become better known to himself and others; that the desire for grace and glory may increasingly be strengthened in him; that hidden sins may be uncovered and future sins prevented; that he be taught tenderness of conscience and a correct and precise observation of his conduct; that he become empty and poor of spirit; that he obtain an aversion to this world and to the pilgrim's life; that he be weaned of external, earthly joy and consolation; that he learn to be fed with tears as the only delicacy of consolation when the Comforter is not present; that on account of these things he may cling to his God all the more firmly. "My soul clings to you; your right hand upholds me" (Ps. 63:8).

Further ends are that God may grant relief in this situation of testing as well as triumph after a complete victory or at least times of refreshment and lovely intervals or periods. "God is faithful, and he will not let you be tempted beyond your strength, but with the temptation will also provide the way of escape, that you may be able to endure it" (1 Cor. 10:13). "But in all these things we are more than conquerors through him who loved us" (Rom. 8:37). "Thanks be to God, who always causes us to triumph in Christ" (2 Cor. 2:14). "Blessed are you who weep now, for you will laugh" (Luke 6:21). "Light dawns for the righteous, and joy for the upright in heart" (Ps. 97:11). "Those who sow in tears reap with shouts of joy" (Ps. 126:5).

Abandonment, however, also serves to make the grace of God, indeed even the smallest crumb and the tiniest feeling of it, all the more precious and pleasant to them, "for the mercy of God is better than life." It is granted so that they may all the more painstakingly preserve the evidences of his favor and thank the Lord all the more fervently for them. It is given so that also the faint and thirsty soul may be flooded by a new stream of consolations, inundated by an entire sea, and thus possess a new heaven while on earth, being prepared to bid the earth farewell and to go to heaven through the valley of the shadow of death. Excellent examples of that heavenly rejoicing and of the sweet elation of the heart following the return of the Bridegroom and restored consolation are narrated by Robert Bolton, first of all with respect to Robert Glover, whose story we shall reproduce here.

After Robert Glover had been condemned by the bishop and was to end his life as a martyr, it happened that two or three days before his death his soul was full of grief and devoid of all spiritual consolation, and he found within himself no trace of the ability and readiness to bear the cross that would soon be laid on him. On the contrary, he found within himself a dullness and numbness of spirit and the absence of all consolation. And since he now privately feared that the Lord had removed his usual grace from him, he complained about this to a certain Augustine, his intimate and faithful friend, to let him know how zealously and sincerely he had called out to the Lord night and day, yet had not received from him any indication or feeling of consolation. But the above-mentioned Augustine spoke to the complainant and admonished him to the effect that he should expect the good pleasure of the Lord with patience, and, though the situation appeared to be very terrifying, he nevertheless exhorted him—because his cause was true and just—to steadfastly uphold the good cause and to prove himself a man, not doubting that the Lord would visit him in due time, filling him with the abundance of his consolations.

And then what happened? The following day when the hour of his martyrdom had struck and he went to the place of execution and saw the pole to which he would be tied, after having prayed the night before with great exertion and vigor and not having felt any spark of joy at all, he unexpectedly and instantly, from that moment on, was filled with the Holy Spirit. This was so real that, clapping his hands, he summoned Augustine to come to him and burst out, "Augustine, he came, he came!" He spoke these words with such great joy and mental proficiency that it seemed he had been delivered from a deadly peril rather than, amid the present pains of death, was about to depart from this life.

A second example is that of a godly woman named Catherine Bretterg. A third is that of a minister of the Word by the name of William Peacock. I cannot help relating here their triumphant words and, as it were, their swansongs[4] because they possibly occur nowhere else in this form and the stories are published only in English.

Thus, Catherine cried out:

> O Lord Jesus! Are you he who prays for me? O blessed, sweetest Savior, how marvelous, how marvelous, how utterly marvelous are your mercies! O that inexpressible love of you who have so graciously dealt with me! O my Lord and my God, your name be praised forever, because you have shown to me the path of life. You, O Lord, hid your face from me for a moment, but you have shown me compassion with an everlasting love (cf. Isa. 54:8). And now, O Lord, your comforting presence has come, you have looked upon your servant with favor and have revealed to her a fullness of joy and consolation. Your name be praised, O Lord my God! Oh, the joy, joy, joy that I feel in my heart! Oh, how marvelous, how marvelous, how utterly marvelous are they! My Father, how merciful and marvelously gracious you are toward me! Yes, Lord, I feel your mercy and am assured of your love; as surely as you are a God of truth, so surely do I know that I am yours, O my Lord and my God! And this my

4. Swans are said to sing a lovely song shortly before their death.

> soul acknowledges, this my soul acknowledges! Praised be God, who has thus consoled me and brought me now into a place that is much lovelier to me than the Garden of Eden. Oh, the joy, oh, the joy, oh, the pleasurable joy that I feel! Praise the Lord for his mercies and for the joy and pleasure that my soul feels to the full. Praise his name forever!

Here are the words of William Peacock after experiencing the first relief following his trial:

> Truly my heart and soul have been far removed and deeply wounded by temptations and irritations of conscience, but I thank God that these have now been largely relieved. So then, it is my desire that I not be marked with the brand of a reprobate. I revoke all the questions and objections I raised and everything that may have tended in that direction. As for any ill-considered words I uttered in my trial, I ask forgiveness for them from a humble heart and from the depths of my soul.

When the light of consolation increasingly dawned and glittered in his heart, he burst out, "I now feel (Praise God!) such great consolation that I do not know by what name to call it." When a bystander asked him whether he still experienced struggle and inner conflict, he answered:

> By no means; it is so little that it is not worth mentioning. If I had five hundred worlds, it would still be a present far too small for such an outcome. The sea is not so full of water, nor the sun so full of light, as the Lord is full of mercies. Indeed, his mercies are ten thousand times greater. What powerful reason I have to praise God's great goodness, God who humbled me or rather exalted me to such a state of honor and glory—wretched miscarriage, poor and pitiful man that I am! The Lord has crowned me with his loving kindness. I am persuaded that he has gifted me with his glorious kingdom. The joy I feel in my heart is incredible.

The ultimate end of these abandonments is the honor of the wisdom, mercy, and power of God revealed in the salvation of his elect in whose weakness he is so powerful and whom he leads to salvation in such a marvelous way—by all kinds of byways and adversities—through hell to heaven, so to speak. Just as the hostility between beloveds may tend to a greater renewal of love, so the Lord our God makes wholesome nourishment out of poison, out of wounds, and out of the most bitter, even hellish pain, the most healing medicines, and from the increase of mitigating evil, his marvelous balm. Thus, the Physician of souls opens the eyes of the blind by smearing mud on them and demonstrates that his justice (to quote Augustine) is the depth of his mercy and his mercy the depth of his justice.

Kinds of Desertion

One can divide desertion as follows: (1) With a view to the kind, desertion can be divided into real so-called afflictions or abandonments—the kind we have dealt with so far—and passing sensations and swiftly disappearing glimmerings that can be caught and noted, like the blush on a face produced by shame and similar sensations. The latter are imperfect abandonments. To this category can be assigned all hasty and confused horrors by which God the Lord as a rule calls people to faith and repentance as with a trumpet sounding from heaven. (2) The circumstances that attend the desertion can be divided into a variety of kinds that can be readily discerned from the concurrence of this illness with one or more of the circumstances. (3) With a view to its degrees, people divide desertion into formidable and less formidable abandonments, into the illness itself and the attack of illness. (4) With a view to duration, people distinguish a longer and a shorter, an ongoing and an occasionally interrupted abandonment, or also one that attacks a person in childhood (so to speak) or in the full adulthood of being a new creature, sometimes not until the end of life or in the hour of death. This last kind occurs frequently. In that case, and by these means, God the Lord wishes to train his champions, now established by grace and being in Christ, not only to the point of sweating but to the point of shedding their blood, and no longer to give them the sweet milk of his consolation but to cause them to drink from the bitter cup of champions and wrestlers. (5) With a view to a person's state, it is divided into the abandonment that comes over persons in the throes and sorrows of their first conversion or rebirth when they have not yet tasted the sweetness of the Lord but are in process of passing from the law to grace and into the abandonment that comes over people who are already converted and have tasted the consolations of God. In the initial conversion, that consolation is withheld so that people do not feel it; in the second, it is withdrawn so that people no longer feel what they used to feel. The latter is much more troublesome than the former, for those who are accustomed to the sweetness of grace suffer more intensely than those who are not yet accustomed to it.

An example of the first kind of abandonment occurred in the life of the excellent theologian Robert Bolton, whom the Lord God first visited over a period of months (as is told in his biography) with this spiritual affliction, which was even intensified by horrible thoughts about God and terrible doubts about the faith. The second kind of abandonment sometimes occurs shortly after conversion and after having acquired the firstfruits of consolation. It was experienced with great intensity by Luther so "that there was neither any natural warmth, nor blood, nor voice left in him," as the Reformer attested in a letter to Melanchthon. This letter can be found in a biography on Luther written by Justus Jonas and later published by Melchior Adamus.

Sometimes this kind of abandonment occurs a long time after conversion, and, as we said earlier, it is more frequent. We encounter it most often in outstanding ministers of God, in those who are pillars of the church and excel in knowledge and godliness.

The question arises at this point whether the abandonments of the elect can also happen in very young children who are called early in life. The answer is that since experience teaches that the practice of faith and conversion, in keeping with the use of the intellect, grows and matures gradually, it is not at all strange that faith of whatever quality it may be, or this disposition to faith, is subject to eclipses, collapses, and faintnesses.

Total Desertion

Contrasting with this abandonment, and in view of the absence of it, is the total withholding of all saving grace, both as it concerns its root and its fruit, in the case of hypocrites and all those who are not saved. Included here is the sudden, impermanent, and totally unfruitful dismay of the natural conscience in unconverted people, with which they frequently—with tears and an external display of theological learning and some external abstention from their usual sins—flaunt the hearing of God's Word along with church attendance. But like dogs returning to their vomit, they distance themselves from this again and cast off all evidence of humiliation, for when the occasion for this dismay of conscience, that is, illness or the fear of death or any other danger or form of trouble, has passed, that dismay also vanishes. One can find an example of it in Robert Bolton's *Instructions.*

Also opposed to this abandonment is excessive abundance: over-satiation or spiritual intoxication. This occurs when a given person is emotionally satiated to the point of fastidiousness and nausea with the great influx of consolations. The result is that the familiar stimulant for the enjoyment of this food, that is, the spiritual appetite, diminishes.

Remedies

Since until now we have dealt with the nature of this disease, what remains for us is to point out the remedies. There are a number of preventative means and antidotes that can be reduced to the following three chapters. First, all the hindrances and causes that intensify this evil must be removed; second, we must avoid and reject all false remedies; finally, we must take up and use the right remedies.

The hindrances that must be removed are all heresies, all sins, and all those things that we have already summed up under the preceding and external causes, such as the harmful doctrine of the falling away of the saints, of free will and the meritoriousness of good works, and so forth. To this must be added the peril of excessive solitude and depressiveness, things that Luther, the man of God, not incorrectly designated "Satan's bath."

We must avoid false remedies such as (1) earthly comforts in the form of sensual pleasures and enjoyments, vain pastimes, the lessening of activity and the relaxation of zeal for self-mortification, and especially the scrupulous practice of godliness, and so forth, as is taught by practical authors both among us and among the papists. (2) We must not praise the patients too much, elevating them above many other believers, by which it is more or less suggested to them that they must draw peace of conscience and consolation from their own works. (3) We must guard against trivializing this evil as if it did not exist or amount to much or as if it is nothing but a concoction of their own foolishness and pessimistic attitude. (4) We must similarly avoid trivializing sins and an all too ready, general, and undiscerning expansion of the mercy of God. (5) We must guard against a stripped-down version of the commandments: Do this, believe that, tell yourself this, avoid that, reject this or that, and so on, without in the process persuading people that the grace they do not feel, and deny feeling, in themselves is in fact in them. This battering ram must be applied in particular.

The means to be used are part purgative and part restorative. Those of the first kind are the examination of conscience and its relief by the renewal of penitence, along with fasting and prayer. Those of the other kind are: (1) the general means such as the exercise of godliness, both in the home and outside it, diligent exertion in one's daily occupation, keeping company with godly folks, especially the ministers of the Word. These ought above all to be equipped with the gift and art of consolation and to watch over the consciences of the people entrusted to their care in this state *(Helvetic Confession,* chap. 25). Add to this the use of medicines and keeping a diet, if the body has perhaps also been affected, either before the abandonment, or concurrently with it, or later by its influence. (2) The special means are the restorative aids of the consolations composed of the experiences and remembrances of the past, the contemplation of the present, and the desire or yearning for the future, or that which is not yet visible. Let the general remedy be a spiritual yearning accompanied by sorrows. Once this has been found, as it is in all who are truly converted, we can firmly conclude—against all doubts and evil suspicions—that they are in the state of grace, as can be seen from the immovable grounds of Holy Scripture.

Thus, our Savior says, "Blessed are the poor in spirit, for theirs is the kingdom of heaven. Blessed are those who mourn, for they will be comforted. Blessed are the meek, for they will inherit the earth" (Matt. 5:3–5). And "Come to me, all you who are weary and heavy-laden, and I will give you rest" (Matt. 11:28). In Isaiah, God the Lord speaks as follows: "Ho, everyone who thirsts! Come to the waters; and you who have no money, come, buy, and eat! Come, buy wine and milk, without money and without price!" (55:1). Compare this with Psalm 51:16–17: "For you have no delight in sacrifice; if I were to give a burnt offering, you would not be pleased. The sacrifices acceptable to God are a broken spirit; a broken and a contrite heart, O God, you will not despise." (Also, see our *Proof of the Power of Godliness* against Tilenus, part 2, chapter 5.) Among those who have completed the entire work of conversion and tasted the sweetness of the Lord there will also take place the remembrance of the preceding consolations, as in the psalms of David: "I considered the days of old and remembered the years of long ago. I thought of my playing a stringed instrument" (Ps. 77:6–7). Undergirded by the sweetest doctrine of the perseverance of the saints, they can clearly draw their conclusion against all temptations.

Additional Resources

With those who are still in labor on account of their conversion, and hence in transition from "law" to "grace" and from "the spirit of bondage" to "the Spirit of adoption as children," one must proceed in the way Theodore Beza prescribes, for among those people, remembrance does not take place. (See *The Acts of the Conversation at Mompelgard.* Perkins placed his words as a postscript after his *Golden Chain,* and they can be read there.) See further the general way in which to bring about healing in these abandonments and temptations in the work of the aforementioned writers, among whom William Couper, bishop of Galloway, by his clear and concise argumentation, surpasses the others, while Robert Bolton stands out in his succinct and profound proofs and vigorous application. Both of these men have experienced this conflict in their own lives. In orderliness of method and vivid description, William Perkins takes the crown, while John Downame is the one to consult for broad instruction with respect to the disease and the antidote against it, both in general and in particular.

The question concerning general temptations—namely, whether a person so abandoned or tempted in conscience could have true faith and be in the state of grace—is treated (alongside the writers mentioned above) superbly by Richard Sibbes in his treatise *The*

Broken Reed and in his work *The Soul's Conflict and Victory over Itself.* Also, Thomas Goodwin does this in his treatise *The Child of Light Walking in Darkness.* For reasons mentioned earlier, the way and order in which, according to the papists, one may be healed of this disease is very deficient. However, where they do speak correctly, they speak very well.

Aside from the authors cited, John Gerson offers a number of things worth reading in his treatise *Remedy against Faint-heartedness* and in another work entitled *Spiritual Beggary.* But surpassing all others is William of Paris, whose words one of our own men, William Ames, has included as an extract in his second volume of *Cases of Conscience.*

Helpful Suggestions

The nucleus and complete summary of the arguments from which one must proceed when facing the questions, excuses, inferences, and mistaken suspicions of abandoned and spiritually oppressed persons is:

First of all, that this abandonment is a kind of cross and visitation with which the Lord God afflicts his children and only them, as experience and the following Scripture passages clearly show. "Oh, that my vexation were rightly weighed and all my calamity laid in the balances! For then it would be heavier than the sand of the sea; therefore my words are being swallowed up. For the arrows of the Almighty are in me; my spirit drinks their poison. The terrors of God are arrayed against me" (Job 6:2–4). "For you write bitter things against me and make me reap the iniquities of my youth" (Job 13:26). "He has torn me in his wrath and hated me; he has gnashed his teeth at me; my adversary sharpens his eyes against me" (Job 16:9). David, too, speaks this way: "In the days of my trouble, I sought the LORD; in the night my hand was stretched out without wearying; my soul refused to be comforted. When I thought of God, I moaned; if I meditated, my spirit grew faint. You kept my eyelids from closing; I was so troubled, I could not speak" (Ps. 77:2–4). And the bride in the Song of Songs says, "My beloved thrust his hand into the opening, and my inmost being yearned for him.... I opened to my beloved, but my beloved was gone. My soul failed me when he spoke. I sought him but did not find him; I called him, but he gave no answer" (Song of Sol. 5:4, 6).

The second argument is that our Savior himself preceded us in this experience. Of his struggle and abandonment we read, "In his anguish he prayed more earnestly, and his sweat became like great drops of blood falling down on the ground" (Luke 22:44) and "He cried with a loud voice, 'My God, my God, why have you forsaken me?'" (Matt. 27:46).

The third argument is that the reality of faith does not consist in the abundance and feelings of consolation. There are many things we possess although we do not feel them, as, for example, when a person has lost consciousness. "It is the office of faith to believe the things that are invisible, to hope the things delayed, to acknowledge God as Father even when he presents himself as our enemy." So speaks the man of God Luther.

The fourth argument is that God is the author of the cross and that he will provide for us in it and give us a way out. For abandoning us, he by no means abandons us, and although our sins lead us downward, God's mercy lifts us upward. Because he does not forsake us in order that we be forsaken, he seems for the moment to have abandoned us, because he does not want us to be abandoned. In sermon 75 of his work on the *Song of Songs,* Bernard superbly comments, "In my bed night after night I sought him whom my soul loves. The Bridegroom has not returned when the Bride calls him back with cries and prayers. Why not? He wishes to increase her desire, test her affection, and exercise her faculty of love. He is not displeased with her, he is concealing his love."

So, then, it follows from everything that has been taught in the past (1) that those who lean to the sentiments of the Pelagians cannot draw any comfort for the troubled conscience from the foundations of their doctrine; (2) that the doctrine—as though there are promptings and suggestions of the devil that are distinct from the promptings of our flesh, and that we ourselves in no way contribute to them or participate in them—is simply to be rejected and condemned. We say this along with Abernethy, Downame, Bolton, Ames, Perkins, Harpe, Boys, Bonaventure, Albertus Magnus (in his treatise *On Clinging to God*), and other practical authors. This question, thus settled, is very useful in the polemic against certain Remonstrants in disguise. See our *Thersites,* part 3, page 289: "If our flesh does not always cooperate with these promptings, that they are produced by both causes (namely, the devil and our flesh), then it follows that we are free from the sins in question, both in respect to the external torments and the terrors of Satan."

Closing Questions

In conclusion, let us now treat a few special cases.

Must those who feel spiritually weak abstain from participation in the Lord's Supper, from listening to the divine Word and from the prayers, because they think they have no faith or question whether they have any?

Answer: By no means, for God must be sought with constant yearning, also when the feeling of his nearness is not experienced. In addition, it is by these means that the life of the Spirit is maintained, just as we eat food to preserve life, even though we have neither desire nor appetite for it.

How must people be strengthened who say they have no desire or yearning to live close to the Lord or at least doubt whether their desire is a true one?

Answer: Those people must be strengthened by the fact that they have a desire for the desire and a yearning for the yearning, that is, they wish their desire to be true and do their best to make it so, and because, with constant pain and grief, they are tormented on account of their deficiency, and because their desire is not inconstant, detached, superficial, vain, and inactive but firm, constant, right down to the center of their being, inward, and active.

Do those who are afflicted with abandonments also decline in the practice of godliness and the careful custody of their conscience?

Answer: The truth is they very much increase in it, for they concentrate all the powers of their soul to avoid even the slightest sin and to fear God. In short, it is they who preeminently work out their salvation in fear and trembling. Like those who have been deprived of eyesight but whose hearing is all the sharper for it, those who are insensible in this part are the most sensible in all other parts.

How can we best take away from people the opinion or suspicion that they have committed the sin against the Holy Spirit?

Answer: By pointing out to them that they are capable of being sorry for their sins and do request the prayers of others for themselves. Neither of these two can occur if people have sinned against the Holy Spirit. This is evident from Hebrews 6:4–6: "It is impossible to restore again to repentance those who have once been enlightened and have tasted the heavenly gift and have shared in the Holy Spirit and have tasted the goodness of the word of God and the powers of the age to come, and then have fallen away, since to their loss they are crucifying the Son of God all over again and subjecting him to public disgrace." Also see 1 John 5:16: "If anyone sees his brother commit a sin that does not lead to death, he should pray and God will give him life. I am speaking of those whose sin does not lead to death. There is a sin that leads to death. I am not saying that he should pray about that." And Christ says, "And therefore I tell you: every sin and blasphemy will be forgiven people, but the blasphemy against the Holy Spirit will not be forgiven them" (Matt. 12:31).

How must we judge concerning those who, being very heavily tempted in their final death-struggle, have to contend with doubt and despair and yet do not seem to be restored before their decease but depart from here in that condition?

Answer: We must hope for the best concerning them if we can detect any sign of spiritual yearning in them, especially if a profession of faith and a Christian life preceded their demise.

Thus, Perkins, in his treatise on spiritual abandonments, judges concerning a certain Chamberius of Leicester, who in his adversity and illness cried out that he was without hope and damned and died in that state:

> However, let no one brand him as a reprobate. For a single utterance he produced during his conflict, 'Oh, if only I had had a single drop of faith!' must be enough for us, in Christian charity, to hope the best for him. From this we can infer that he had a heart desirous of repenting and believing and therefore indeed had a believing, penitent heart. For God the Lord, at all times but especially in the hour of testing, in accord with his great mercy, counts the will for the deed.

Thus, Perkins judges—along with other theologians, such as Wolfgang Musculus, indeed, even Arminius, and now recently

Godfriedus Udemans in his *Meditations* on Matthew 25, also with respect to Francis Spira. For certainly one must not give credence to their cries or confessions of despair, because that voice is not a voice of credibility or truth but of weakness; it is not making a statement but expressing a doubt. So also are the words of Jeremiah when he says, "You would be in the right, O Lord, if I should lay charges against you. Yet I would speak with you about your justice. Why does the way of the wicked prosper? Why do all the faithless live at ease? You have planted them, and they have taken root; they grow and bring forth fruit. You are always on their lips but far from their hearts" (Jer. 12:1–2). The words of Asaph read, "Surely in vain I have kept my heart clean and washed my hands in innocence. For all day long I have been plagued and am punished every morning" (Ps. 73:13–14). "Will the Lord spurn forever and never again be favorable? Has his steadfast love ceased forever? Are his promises at an end for all time? Has God forgotten to be gracious? Has he in anger withheld his compassion?" (Ps. 77:7–9). And Job says, "Why do you hide your face and count me as your enemy?" (Job 13:24). On this, see in greater detail our treatise against Tilenus. Truly, like these writers, so also William Peacock and Catherine Bretterg uttered words of despair, like people devoid of hope, as Robert Bolton tells us.

On the other hand, they can also be restored and triumph over their temptation a moment after the trial in question, or at least before their decease, although they could not make it known because of the fainting, failing powers of their body, either by voice or gesture, for the soul, even when it no longer functions or feels externally, has its own internal operations.

Finally, even if it were the case that they were not restored inwardly before their death but departed during a severe attack of insensibility and temptation, nothing certain could be concluded about their final and total impenitence and unbelief. This could be done only if it were first established that actual, particular, and always ensuing repentance and remorse (renewed after every sin) is absolutely and indispensably necessary to salvation.

Johannes Hoornbeeck (1617–66)

Spiritual Desertion

by Johannes Hoornbeeck

1

There is nothing new in the fact, and therefore it is not surprising, that different authors write about one and the same subject—especially when its importance is such that the judgment and considerations of many people are required. In one of Augustine's books entitled *The Trinity,* the author highly commends the practice of many authors writing about the same subject, provided it is done in differing ways. Nor has anyone ever faulted Cyprian because, reading daily in the works of Tertullian his teacher, he wrote about the same things as he. He even frequently took over Tertullian's reservations and reasons, as, for example, when he wrote about "patience" and in another book about the "attire of daughters." In the Talmud of the Jews, a certain Rabbi writes, "He who forbids a pupil to express his opinion is like a person who wants to deprive him of his parents' inheritance; for it is written," he said, "Moses charged us with the law, as an inheritance of the assembly of Jacob" (Deut. 33:4).

Spiritual desertion, or abandonments, on which I have been asked to express my opinion, is, above all other topics, worth being treated by many authors, the more because the ancients have said little about the topic other than under the general heading of "Difficulties" or "Trials and Temptations" and a little in their commentaries on the Song of Solomon.

What spiritual abandonments and the circumstances attending them are can be rightly understood only by those who know and possess the Spirit of God. To others, who live apart from and without God, "being aliens from the commonwealth of Israel and strangers to the covenants of promise, having no hope" (Eph. 2:12), and have the nerve to say, "We have not even heard that there is a Holy Spirit" (Acts 19:2), it seems that what is said here about spiritual abandonments is a vain dream and farfetched fantasy. But also those who by the grace and power of God have already been born again, who have the Spirit of God dwelling within them and live by the grace of God, often fall into this condition and cannot themselves say and explain what it really is and what they will call it. In that case, their condition is like that of one who becomes sick but does not know the nature of the illness. In the case of many, too, there is a great lack of expertise in how they must deal with people who have suffered these attacks, and because frequently, mistaking one thing for another, they fail to understand the condition of the sick person and the nature of the illness, they also fail, slightly or greatly, in their approach to healing. Hence, both the difficulty of this subject and the necessity of instructing others, particularly our students who are in training for the ministry of the church and the care of souls, are reason enough for us to write on the subject, even though our highly respected teacher and colleague Dr. Voetius has already done this.

Furthermore, we encourage everyone diligently to contribute to this discussion everything he knows that may furnish aid and comfort to those souls who would readily give or abandon everything to receive instruction and comfort amid such a soul struggle and such anxiety, more than those who, suffering from some physical illness or pain, are anxious and eager for help or alleviation of pain.

They are called "spiritual desertion," or "abandonments"—the most severe trials the soul may suffer here below, trials most resembling hellish fears and sorrows, when it pleases God to take his children to heaven past the brink of hell. "My inward parts are in turmoil and are never still," says Job (30:27). "My heart pounds. My strength has failed me," says David (Ps. 38:10). "Deserted and distressed in spirit," Isaiah concludes (Isa. 54:6). And Jeremiah indicates it is a heavy burden: "What burden? That I shall abandon you, says the Lord" (Jer. 23:33), just as he said of himself, "There was in my heart as it were a burning fire shut up in my bones, and I made an effort to bear it but could not" (Jer. 20:9).

It is a heaviness in the soul about spiritual matters. But since we call it "abandonments" or "desertion," and since this indicates some kind of privation, this expression can be understood only by reference to its opposite, hence, by indicating the good concerning whose privation we are speaking. We can no more understand what darkness is without some notion of light, or what blindness is without the experience of vision than we can understand what "spiritual abandonments" are without first recalling the grace whose lack or deprivation is indicated by this term. One may describe the grace of God either as the grace and favor of God by which God aims at our well-being and all the good he intends for us, or as the grace that is within us, consisting of all the benefits (especially spiritual benefits, which we also have in mind here) that we have received from God. With respect to the former, God is usually called "gracious" in Scripture (Exod. 33:19).

On account of the latter, it is said of us that we obtain "grace" from God (thus, in Romans 1:7, "grace and peace," and in other letters, such as 1 Peter 4:10, "manifold grace," and in John 1:16, "grace for grace." Now, of the grace granted to the elect, it must be said first that faith, hope, and love are its pith and essence; second, as a consequence of that grace there is a feeling of peace, comfort, joy in God, and salvation.

The first, that is, the essence of that grace, is definitely necessary and always present. It is granted to all the elect and remains in them. They can never lose it. It is, as John puts it, "the anointing which remains" (1 John 2:27) and "his seed remains in him," or as we read elsewhere, "imperishable seed" (1 Peter 1:23), "the implanted word that has roots" (James 1:21; cf. Matt. 13:21).

But the second, the feeling of grace, is subject to change: it can be darkened, lessened, yes, even removed for a time, like the feeling of life in the case of an unconscious person, or a tree in winter, or a flame that dances on a fire. Thus, also faith and the Spirit will always remain in the soul, but their effect or operation in it sometimes ceases. Just as those who believe in God and Christ (John 14:1) take delight in God, in whom they believe, and in the fact that they believe, through which they gain a sense of the priceless grace and gifts granted them (which, if they were not aware that they believed they could not delight in), so here too feeling follows faith, the feeling of faith that produces peace in the soul. Feeling the inworking of God in whom they believe, they inevitably derive inexpressible and abundant delight from this fact, because in a soul that comes to him in faith, God inevitably pours out torrents of his sensible favor, glory, and heavenly joy. What, on the other hand, is the condition of the soul when God abandons it? God does not, to be sure, take all his grace and favor away from that soul. He does not totally deprive it of all saving gifts and the gifts necessary to salvation, for as we read in 2 Samuel 7:15, the Lord says, "I will not take my steadfast love from him, as I took it from Saul," that is, with respect to those general benefits that are also given to others outside the circle of the elect, as Saul says to Samuel, "I am in great distress, for God has departed from me" (1 Sam. 28:15).

But those whom God has once for all accepted in Christ Jesus as his children and favored with the saving gifts and grace, he never abandons totally, "For the Lord will not abandon his people for his great name's sake, because it has pleased the Lord to make you a people for himself" (1 Sam. 12:22). Nehemiah 9:31 says, "Nevertheless, in your great mercies you did not make an end of them or forsake them, for you are a gracious and merciful God." For the same reason, God does not now abandon the person here with an act of eternal and total abandonment, for he has received that person as his child; and even though he sins and deserves to be totally abandoned by God, yet God continues to be gracious and merciful to him. He has said after all, "I will never leave you or forsake you" (Heb. 13:5), while in Isaiah we read, "Can a woman forget her nursing child or show no compassion for the child of her womb? Even these may forget, yet I will never forget you" (49:15).

Then what does it mean when it is said that God has abandoned a soul? It means that, excepting the grace necessary to salvation, he withdraws from a soul with respect to its feeling and joy; that he no longer allows the soul to savor his grace and friendship as before; that he does not overwhelm that soul with heavenly consolations and joy as in the past. As a result of this withdrawal, the soul no longer has a sense of any grace of God within itself and fails to find its rest in it, while it cannot delight in anything, whether in religious exercises or whatever it is occupied with, since it misses the ordinary experience of rest and joy that it used to enjoy in God and his blessings. The soul then exists in a state of pitiable gloom and dryness. Instead of rest it experiences nothing but unrest and despondency; in fact, it is in conflict, conflict even with God, who, though he formerly comforted it, now refuses to cause his gracious face to shine upon it and is angry with it. God abandons and defeats the soul so that it has to cry out, "Do not be a terror to me; you are my refuge in the day of disaster" (Jer. 17:17). Storms arise in the soul: "Deep calls to deep in the roar of your waterfalls; all your waves and breakers have swept over me" (Ps. 42:7). "The waters have come up to the soul. I have sunk in the miry depths where there is no foothold. I have come into the deep waters, and the flood engulfs me" (Ps. 69:2–3). It speaks like David in Psalm 55: "My heart is in anguish within me, and the terrors of death assail me. Fear and trembling have beset me; horror has overwhelmed me. I said, 'Oh, that I had the wings of a dove! I would fly away and be at rest—I would flee far away and lodge in the desert'" (vv. 4–7).

This is how these people are whose soul is disturbed and in anguish before God; they attempt to escape from everything to seek solitude. Everything they see, hear, and think reminds them over and over of their evil and makes it worse. "I was afraid of my own room; it was as if even this room knew what I was thinking," says Jerome. God stands at a distance and when the enemy says, "God has abandoned him," the soul cries out, "O God, be not far from me; my God, hasten to my aid. Show them your back and not your face, as it is written in Jeremiah: 'I will show them my back, not my face in the day of their calamity'" (18:17). "How long, O Lord? Will you forget me forever? How long will you hide your face from me?" (Ps. 13:1). "O Lord, why do you stand far off? Why do you hide yourself in times of trouble?" (Ps. 10:1). It is a hiding like that of which we read in the Song of Solomon: "Behold! There he stands behind our wall, gazing in at the windows, looking through the lattice" (2:9). It is a "leaving" in the sense in which a husband and wife leave their parents. It does not mean they totally reject their parents; they only leave father and mother while continuing to feel affection for them. Similarly, it is said of Christ that he was going away from the world, though he continues to remain with us even to the end of the world.

Thus, it is also said of the Lord that he had departed from Samson. This referred, however, only to the power that had left him; the Lord never withdrew his saving grace from Samson, as we learn from Hebrews 11, where the apostle counts him among the believers and redeemed of the Old Testament. Paul writes in the same way in his second letter to Timothy: "At my first defense no one came to my support, but all deserted me" (4:16), a statement by which he does not mean to say that they all withdrew their friendship from him but that they did not stand firm and did not offer him this deed of sacred fellowship, which is why he writes, "did not *come to my support.*" So also here. It is not that God totally abandons and rejects the soul in such a state, that he completely withdraws his grace and favor from it; the case is only that he does not show his favor as before. It is with respect to the feeling or experience of his grace that he leaves the soul and thus withdraws from it; yet he nevertheless—even in the midst of this abandonment—remains its God. It accords with the prayer, "Do not forsake me, O Lord; O my God, do not be far from me" (Ps. 38:21). God, as it were, recedes a little but will return to his place (Hosea 5:15). Like a child whose mother for a moment lets go of the child's hand or moves a few feet away and immediately the child becomes scared, so also it is with the soul. The truth is—though the child does not know it and thinks it has been abandoned—the heart of the mother has not changed but remains the same. It is like the love between a husband and a wife that always remains, even though the husband sometimes has to leave his wife for a time. As a result, the two all the more intensely feel their love for one another. So it is with Christ, who, following his—mutually felt—sensible fellowship, withdraws from the church for a short time. Yet his heart continues to burn with love for her, even more than she can fathom or than her own heart can yearn for Christ.

In Song of Solomon, chapter 3, we read how Christ avoided his bride, the church, and what happens before she finds him again. "Upon my bed at night I sought him whom my soul loves; I sought him but did not find him" (v. 1). Here, accordingly, we observe three things: (1) that Christ was not with her but had departed from her; (2) that she therefore looked for him; (3) that she did not immediately find him. In chapter 5, Christ comes to her, filled with an assortment of the gifts of the Spirit, to tell her that it was on account of her disgraceful neglect that she had not let him in. "Listen! My beloved is knocking. 'Open to me, my sister, my love, my dove, my perfect one; for my head is wet with dew, my locks with the drops of the night'" (5:2). Thus, he comes at his own initiative and with abundant blessings to pour them out upon her, the unworthy one. But what happens? "I have," says she, "put off my skirt. How can I put it on again? I have washed my feet. How can I soil them again?" Whereupon she continues: "My beloved pulled his hand from the opening, and my inmost being yearned for him. I arose to open to my beloved, and my hands dripped with myrrh, my fingers with liquid myrrh, upon the handles of the bolt. I opened to my beloved, but my beloved had turned and was gone. My soul failed me when he spoke. I sought him but did not find him; I called him, but he did not answer" (vv. 3–6). And what happens to her as she searches for him? With reference to others, we read in verse 7: "Making their rounds in the city, the sentinels found me; they beat me, they wounded me, they took away my veil, those sentinels on the walls." But with reference to herself, we read in the following verse: "I adjure you, O daughters of Jerusalem, if you find my beloved, what will you tell him? Tell him this: 'I am faint with love.'" And Christ witnesses to his love for her: "You have stolen my heart, my sister, my bride; you have stolen my heart"; and concerning their return to each other, when she becomes in his eyes as one who finds peace, we read in 3:4: "When I had gone a short distance past them [the sentinels], I found him whom my soul loves. I held him and would not let him go."

Gregory says, "As quickly as he had gone, however, he returned; and to keep her holy soul from being too long away from her beloved and becoming estranged, he shot into her hungry soul by his word and entering it caused it to melt." And in Augustine we read:

> It is with such enchantments that she calls the bridegroom. The Lord, whose eyes are upon the righteous and whose ears are open to their prayers, not even waiting till they are finished, drops by, hastily entering, and soon, filled with the dew of his heavenly sweetness, speeds to the longing soul and refreshes her, the weary one, with precious ointment, nourishes the hungry one, makes fruitful the dry and causes her to forget the earthly, so that, forgetting herself, she is marvelously strengthened by him. He makes her lively, yes, even the sober one drunk [with love].

In the same way, we are given a lively account of the entire state and inner meaning of this matter in the Twenty-Second Psalm. At the very outset already we read, "My God, my God, why have you forsaken me?"

Since we have specifically derived the term *abandonments* from these words, it should be profitable, for a better understanding of our subject, to examine this psalm in somewhat greater detail. The state and condition of such a soul is indicated by the fact that it is abandoned by God, and that in two ways: (1) that the soul in its invocational petitions was not heard by God; and (2) that the soul, which speaks here from a situation of urgent distress, was not helped by God. "Why have you forsaken me? Why are you so far from helping me, from the words of my groaning? O my God, I cry by day, but you do not answer" (Ps. 22:1–2). This, too, is the reason why the speaker has no rest and complains, "I am poured out like water, and all my bones are out of joint; my heart is like wax; it is melted within my breast. My strength is dried up like a potsherd, and my tongue sticks to the roof of my mouth; you laid me in the dust of death" (vv. 14–15). Hence, he is despised and mocked. We read, "But I am a worm and no man, scorned by others and despised by the people. All who see me mock at me; they make mouths at me; they shake their heads, saying, 'He has committed his cause to the LORD; let him deliver—let him rescue the one in whom he delights'" (vv. 6–8).

Now, note how he conducts himself in that state. Despite all this, he delights in God (v. 8); he trusts in God, saying, "My God, my God" and in verse 10, "Since my mother bore me you have been my God"; while in verse 19 he calls God "my strength." He always praises and honors God: "Yet you are holy, enthroned on the praises of Israel" (v. 3); "from you will come my praise in the great congregation" (v. 25). He prays constantly: "I cry by day and by night" (v. 2). The central content of his prayer is expressed in verse 19: "But you, O LORD, do not be far from me"; in my abandonment "come quickly to my aid"; while also in verse 11 he had prayed, "Do not be far from me." As his reasons for his praying, he offers the following: trouble was near, and he was utterly helpless (v. 11); and in verses 12 and 18, he expands on this theme when he says, "Many bulls encircle me," and so on.

In reading these verses, one must not lose sight of the fact that this material relates to the persecutions David endured, but even more to the suffering of Christ. As the reasons for having his prayers heard by God, he refers to the example of the fathers: "In you our ancestors trusted; they trusted, and you delivered them. To you they cried and were saved; in you they trusted and were not put to shame" (vv. 4–5). They trusted you; they cried out to you; they were not put to shame. He further refers to the gracious actions that God had always maintained with him; God always preserved him and commanded him to trust in him: "It was you who took me from the womb; you have made me trust you on my mother's breast" (v. 9). In the following verse, he witnesses that he also did this: "On you I was cast from my birth, and since my mother bore me you have been my God" (v. 10). Now he also makes vows: "I will pay my vows before those who fear him" (v. 25). And the end of all this is rescue, thanksgiving, and the instruction of others.

Mention of rescue is made in verse 24: "For he did not despise or abhor the afflictions of the afflicted, nor did he hide his face from me; but he heard when I cried out to him." He was heard and helped—matters about which he complained just moments before. And in the certain hope of such a rescue he speaks even before he has been rescued.

Mention of thanksgiving is made in verses 22 and 25: "I will tell of your name to my brothers; in the midst of the congregation I will praise you."

We find the instruction and exhortation of others in verses 23 and 26: "You who fear the Lord, praise him; and you offspring of Jacob, glorify him; and stand in awe of him, all you offspring of Israel. . . . The meek will eat and be satisfied."

From this description it should be plain to all how this psalm precisely details the state of the abandoned in all its parts and how we may draw wisdom and consolation from it in this respect. This will prove to be the case in even greater detail from what will be said further. In this connection, let the reader compare Psalms 38, 77, and 88.

This, then, is how things are with the subject of spiritual abandonments. In this connection, we will comment on three things:

1. the abandonment as such
2. the difficulties that arise from it for the abandoned soul
3. the conflict that often arises in the soul as a result and continually furnishes work for it so as to spawn continual unrest

1. The abandonment in itself. This is something we have already discussed. The question here is whether it is not actually indicative of sin for the person so afflicted. Since we are told to be always joyful and to delight in God, to be always active in believing and through this activity to taste God's goodness, is not this abandonment, during which these things do not take place, in fact a sin for the person so afflicted?

In reply, we note that this abandonment, if indeed it comes over the soul from God and he denies to it the feeling of his favor, is nothing other than the chastisement that a person undergoes. In that case, it is not a sin on account of which he must suffer. It is true, however, that his sin is probably and usually an additional element here, and that in three ways:

(1) The cause of this abandonment is very often his sin. "The Lord is with you, while you are with him. If you seek him, he will be found by you, but if you abandon him, he will abandon you" (2 Chron. 15:2). In Isaiah we read, "But you have rejected your people, the house of Jacob, because they are full of wickedness" (2:6). Thus says the Lord, "Where is your mother's bill of divorce with which I put her away? . . . Why, when I came, was there no man? When I called, was there no one to answer?" (Isa. 50:1–2). For the same reason, Ezra answered the king, "The hand of our God is for good upon all who seek him, and the power of his wrath is against all who forsake him" (8:22). Fitting, especially for our purpose, is what Job testifies: "For you write bitter things against me and make me inherit the iniquities of my youth" (13:26). "My transgression is sealed up in a bag, and you pack my iniquity together" (14:17). Gregory the Great describes what is happening here: "The things people regarded as being small when they were done are now found to be very burdensome."

(2) Add to this his sin of omission and neglect of the exercises and duties that were necessary for his consolation and redemption. He does not exercise and apply as he ought the faith and whatever other grace he received from God.

(3) From this follows many kinds of sin, which are accompanied by great unbelief and disobedience, so that the soul refuses to be comforted and in its haste speaks like David: "I am cut off from your sight" (Ps. 31:22).

2. The heavy burden that arises from abandonment. The suffering and the heavy burden that result from this abandonment are very bitter to the soul. They are a great blow that strikes it, a painful breach that thus arises. The soul then complains like Job: "Oh, that my sorrow were weighed and all my calamity laid in the balances! For then it would be heavier than the sand of the sea; therefore my words have been swallowed up. For the arrows of the Almighty are in me; my spirit drinks their poison; the terrors of God are arrayed against me" (6:2–4). "Look at me and be appalled, and lay your hand upon your mouth. When I think of it I am dismayed, and shuddering seizes my flesh" (21:5–6; cf. Psalms 38, 77, 88).

Why is it that this burden is so great and unbearable to the soul that it contorts itself, bends over, and groans? This has three causes.

(1) This evil strikes only the soul, the most sensitive and vital part in a person. It is not a burden that seizes the body and *thereby* causes pain to the soul; it strikes only the soul, the spirit of a person. From this one can readily infer whence it is that this suffering is so severe. Just as the good that is located in the soul is more splendid than that which is located in the body, so also the bad is all the more serious depending on whether it is mental or physical. After all, our body would have no feeling of distress if it were not for the soul, which imparts feeling to the body. Imagine then how sensitive and painful it must be when the soul itself, which is the origin of feeling, is so afflicted! In the body, one area is more sensitive than another, depending on whether more sensitive nerves run through it and the soul produces more feeling there. Above all, how powerful the life and the feeling of the soul itself must be when the soul alone is so afflicted, weighted down, and tormented! One sees it in melancholy people whose soul is so stunned by vague uncertain fear or thoughts that they have almost no feeling for anything other than their burden: "A cheerful heart is a good medicine, but a downcast spirit dries up the bones," says Solomon (Prov. 17:22). "A man's spirit will endure sickness, but a broken spirit, who can lift it up?" (Prov. 18:14).

(2) This evil comes immediately, wholly, and solely from God, so that the soul has to deal with no one other than he and has him against itself. "When he is quiet, who can condemn? When he hides his face, who can behold him?" says Elihu (Job 34:29). While Job himself testifies, "God has made my heart faint; the Almighty has

terrified me" (23:16). Naomi said to her neighbors, "Do not call me Naomi. Call me Mara, for the Almighty has dealt very bitterly with me" (Ruth 1:20). Everyone who knows what God is knows and feels what a dreadful thing it is to fall into the hands of the living God (Heb. 10:31) and to be apprehended and afflicted by him.

(3) A third reason why the soul suffers so under this burden arises from the fact that it strikes at a person's most precious possession, that is, his soul's salvation. Not that a person loses salvation here, but he no longer feels anything of it. It is nothing but darkness in his soul—as if the soul finds itself perpetually in hell. "Indeed, I do not know," says Bernard, "whether the soul would not rather suffer the torments of hell for a time than lose the sweetness it has once tasted." The suffering is all the heavier to the degree that one has the more intensely feasted spiritually. Seneca already observed this phenomenon: "It is most distressful to lose riches after having enjoyed them in the past." The sensible taste of God's favor was life for the soul, indeed, better than life, for David says, "Your loving-kindness is better than life" (Ps. 63:3), and in another psalm he declares, "His favor is for a lifetime" (Ps. 30:5). To be without this favor is more bitter than death. "Because I have said these things to you, sorrow has filled your hearts," said Christ to his disciples after he had spoken to them about his departure (John 16:6).

There are two things here that oppress the soul: the loss of the good and the feeling of the opposite evil. Since our focus here is God and the abandoned soul, the lost good is that this soul loses—in God—the feeling of his grace and in consequence—in itself—the feeling of its salvation. The opposing evil, on the other hand, consists of the feeling of God's heavy hand and wrath against the soul and the consequent feeling of damnation upon itself. Earlier we remarked that all this does not take away the whole of God's grace and that the soul's salvation can nevertheless still be present. "He does not abandon to be abandoned but rather *not* to be abandoned, and therefore seems to abandon because he does not want to abandon," someone has noted. "For this devout person the departure and lack of this favor is the most painful and prime component of his burden." "Has God forgotten to be gracious? Has he in anger shut up his compassion?" complains Asaph (Ps. 77:9).

Asaph is thereby saying, first, I am as one spurned, and hence, I am now oppressed by the feeling as though God's wrath rests on me. And now he asks, "Will the Lord spurn forever and never again be favorable?" (v. 7). And Job, groaning under the heavy pressure of not only God's hand on his poor, abandoned soul but also his numerous physical torments and ailments, laments, "Your hands shaped me and made me. Will you now turn and destroy me?" (10:8). "Withdraw your hand far from me, and stop frightening me with your terrors" (13:21). "Have pity on me, my friends, have pity, for the hand of God has struck me" (19:21). And David cries out, "For your arrows have pierced me, and your hand has come down upon me" (Ps. 38:2). "O Lord, do not rebuke me in your anger or chasten me in your wrath" (Ps. 38:1). God's hand and God's wrath upon one's soul: These are the consequences of God's turning away and abandoning the soul. Then the soul says with David, "Do not hide your face from me, do not turn your servant away in anger" (Ps. 27:9); or with Job, "He has kindled his wrath against me" (19:11). Heman testifies in Psalm 88, "Your wrath lies heavily upon me; you have overwhelmed me with all your waves" (v. 7). "Your wrath has swept over me; your terrors have destroyed me" (v. 16). In Isaiah, God's hiding and anger are joined together: "I hid myself and was angry" (57:17). Similarly, the Lord says to Moses with regard to his people Israel, "Thus my anger will be kindled against them in that day, and I will forsake them" (Deut. 31:17).

Having discussed the act of abandonment on God's part and the burden that results from it, we now come to the third point, where we will note the state of the spiritually abandoned:

3. The spiritual conflict that, in consequence, arises in the soul—it is a constant and vehement conflict, even to the point of blood, and that in several ways.

(1) With God himself. Listen to Job complain about this: "Am I the sea, or a sea monster, that you put me under guard? When I say, 'My bed will comfort me, my couch will ease my complaint,' then you frighten me with dreams and terrify me with visions.... If I have sinned, what have I done to you, O watcher of men? Why have you made me your target? Have I become a burden to you?... You hunt me like a lion and again display your awesome power against me" (Job 7:12–14, 20; 10:16). David laments, "Deep calls to deep in the roar of your waterfalls; all your waves and breakers have swept over me" (Ps. 42:7). "Remove your scourge from me; I

am overcome by the blows of your hand" (Ps. 39:10). Asaph, in Psalm 77, utters the sigh, "When I remembered you, O God, I groaned; if I mused, my spirit grew faint" (v. 3), while Heman says in Psalm 88, "Your wrath has swept over me; your terrors destroy me" (v. 16).

(2) The abandoned have conflict with the devil, who also tempted Christ. Like David's enemies, the devil speaks to the soul: "God has forsaken him; pursue and seize him, for there is none to deliver him" (Ps. 71:11). In that case, following the hidden ways of his wisdom, God somewhat relaxes the devil's control over the soul, as we find in Jeremiah: "I have forsaken my house; I have abandoned my heritage; I have given the beloved of my soul into the hands of her enemies" (12:7), where it is now daily assaulted, shaken, and sifted. Its experience is like that of Peter, to whom the Lord said, "Simon, Simon, Satan demanded to have you that he might sift you like wheat" (Luke 22:31), namely, when God, referring to the soul, said to the devil, "Behold, he is in your hand" (cf. Job 1:12).

(3) The abandoned have to fight with people, against their mistaken judgments, backbiting, taunts, grudges, contempt, slander, persecution, and the like. Listen to Job: "He has alienated my brothers from me; my acquaintances are completely estranged from me. My kinsmen have gone away; my friends have forgotten me. My guests and my maidservants count me a stranger; they look upon me as an alien. I call my servant, but he does not answer, though I beg him with my own mouth. My breath is offensive to my wife; I am loathsome to my own brothers. Even young children despise me; when I rise, they talk against me. All my intimate friends abhor me, and those whom I loved have turned against me" (19:13–19). "And now I have become their song; I am a byword to them" (30:9). In Psalm 42, David laments, "As with a deadly wound in my body, my adversaries taunt me, while they say to me continually 'Where is your God?'" (v. 10). Heman testifies, "You have taken from me my closest friends and have made me repulsive to them" (Ps. 88:8), while in Isaiah we read, "We considered him stricken by God, smitten by him, and afflicted" (53:4).

(4) The abandoned must battle with themselves, since all day long their conscience does nothing but accuse, convict, and condemn, thus squelching faith and grace. "Evildoers without number encircle me" (Ps. 22:16). "My iniquities have seized me for not being

able to see; they are more numerous than the hairs of my head, and my heart has abandoned me" (Ps. 40:12). "My iniquities have gone over my head; they weigh like a burden too heavy for me" (Ps. 38:4).

I will not discuss the fact that often, indeed commonly, the body is also assailed and racked with illnesses and torments, as Job was with ulcerating sores from the soles of his feet to the top of his skull. "You have shriveled me up, which is a witness against me, and my gauntness has risen up against me; it testifies to my face" (Job 16:8); "My skin turns black and falls from me, and my bones burn with heat" (30:30). David laments, "Day and night your hand was heavy upon me; my strength was sapped as in the heat of summer" (Ps. 32:4); "Because of your wrath there is no health in my body; my bones have no soundness because of my sin" (Ps. 38:3); "When you chasten a man with rebukes for sin, you consume like a moth all that is charming about him" (Ps. 39:11). And Heman testifies, "My soul is full of trouble, and my life draws near the grave. . . . My eyes are dim with grief" (Ps. 88:3, 9).

The effects of this condition are:

(1) The soul laments and pitifully groans concerning its breach from within and pertaining to its distress, despondency, fears, and anxieties so that it clamors like a crane or moans like a dove (Isa. 38:14). It says with Job, "For sighing comes to me instead of bread; my groans pour out like water" (3:24). "Does a wild donkey bray when it has grass, or the ox low over its fodder?" (6:5). Thus, the soul indicates that its groaning is not without cause. And, like Job, it continues, "I will speak out in the anguish of my spirit. I will complain in the bitterness of my soul" (7:11). "My face is red with weeping; deep shadows ring my eyes" (16:16). "God's hand is heavy in spite of my groaning" (23:2). "I stand up in the assembly and cry for help" (30:28). With David it testifies, "I pour out my complaint before his face. I tell my trouble before him" (Ps. 142:2). Where others laugh, it weeps, and their joy is the soul's sadness. "You may play, Rufinus," said emperor Theodosius to his courtier on such an occasion, "because you do not feel my trouble. I, on the other hand, sigh and weep over my grief that, while servants and beggars are admitted in the church, the church and heaven are closed to me." In such a state, the soul experiences what David did when he said, "My tears have been my food day and night" (Ps. 42:3), or what

Asaph felt in Psalm 80: "You have fed them with the bread of tears; you have made them drink tears by the bowlful" (v. 5).

(2) The soul desires and hopes with a steady desire, a serious expectation and hope—with outstretched necks, as it were—"for the times of refreshing from the Lord" (cf. Acts 3:19), for "the dawn from on high" (Luke 1:78), so as yet with joy to "draw water from the wells of salvation" (Isa. 12:3). It is the situation of which Psalm 42 speaks: "As the deer pants for streams of water, so my soul pants for you, O God! My soul thirsts for God, for the living God. When shall I come and meet with God?" (vv. 1–2). Augustine says, "That is what I thirsted for, 'to come and meet with.' I thirsted on my journey. I thirsted in the course of my progress. I will be satisfied when I come. But when shall I come?" The psalmist expresses this desire of the soul when he says, "Our soul waits for the Lord; he is our help and shield" (Ps. 33:20). "O God, you are my God, earnestly I seek you; my soul thirsts for you, my body longs for you, in a dry and weary land where there is no water" (Ps. 63:1). Thus, the soul lies open and agape. Jeremiah says, "Wild donkeys stand on the barren heights and pant like jackals" (14:6).

(3) The soul, aside from longing, also searches. In every way possible, it diligently searches for a blessed outcome, indeed, to find him again whom it lost. Thus, Asaph says, "When I was in distress, I sought the Lord; at night I stretched out untiring hands" (Ps. 77:2). It seeks nothing other than God; it values nothing other than his favor. It says with the bride, "I seek him whom my soul loves" (Song of Sol. 3:2). What she has is not enough for her until she finds her beloved. She witnesses with Asaph, "Whom have I in heaven but you? And earth has nothing I desire besides you" (Ps. 73:25), or with Isaiah the prophet, "Oh, that you would rend the heavens and come down" (64:1), or with the suffering Job, "As for me, is my complaint against man?" (21:4). All its desire is directed to God alone; it longs only for his grace; nothing else can satisfy it, no world, no worlds, indeed, not even heaven, except insofar as it finds God there. "There my thirst is assuaged; I indeed admire and praise these things—but thirst? No, I only thirst for him who made them," says Augustine. In that respect, he was like David, of whom we read the testimony, "Your lovingkindness is better than life" (Ps. 63:3). Indeed, the soul would rejoice if it could enjoy just one little crumb from God's table, a drop of his consolation, a ray of his love.

As the martyr John Bradford said to the chancellor, "I have a heartfelt desire for the mercy of God; truly, the mercy of the Lord is better and more precious to me than my own life. Life in God's wrath and disfavor is more bitter than death. Equally, death with God's favor and grace is life itself." Or as another martyr, Frans Verlut, put it in the year 1562: "The grace of Christ has such power that it effects great joy in the person who has received only the tiniest drop of it; for it is living water and those who taste only a little of it will never thirst again."

This is the opposition of the abandoned and his abandonment that often comes upon him as suddenly and unexpectedly as a thunderstorm. "When I looked for good," says Job, "evil came, and when I waited for light, darkness came" (30:26). "What I feared has come upon me; what I dreaded has happened to me" (3:25). "As for me, I said in my prosperity," witnesses David, "I shall never be moved. By your favor, O Lord, you had established me as a strong mountain, but when you hid your face, I was dismayed" (Ps. 30:6–7). So also it went with Asaph. When he no longer felt the gracious presence of God, he said, "This is my grief" (Ps. 77:10). And in Psalm 88, Heman declares that he had had to endure these afflictions from his youth and had been close to death (v. 15).

There is nothing in the world that can quiet the soul, nor can the world itself do it. It is as a martyr put it to King Charles when in 1557 he was offered a large and rich canonry: "You do know, don't you, that the lust of the world cannot quiet the heart of man when his conscience is disturbed?" As great as the treasure of peace of mind is (as Guido de Brès put it at the end of his life, "What a precious comfort a good conscience is"), so great is the evil and burden of an embattled and uneasy soul. "It is not hard," says Thomas à Kempis, "to spurn human consolation if only the divine is present; but certainly something really large occurs when someone can do without both human and divine consolation." And Augustine says, "Of all afflictions nothing is harder for the soul than the indictment of a man's conscience concerning his sins."

Finally, it remains for us to answer the question, To what end does God the Lord visit his elect, that is, his dearest children, with such heavy assaults and abandonments, and what good does it do?

We cannot state everything here that is deserving of comment, nor can we mention all the reasons why it pleases God the Lord to deal thus with us. We will confine ourselves to the most obvious and important.

First, spiritual abandonment takes place to test us, that it may be all the clearer what is present in our heart: our sincerity and uprightness by which we cling to God and cannot abandon him even when he turns away from us and seems to abandon us. "My soul clings to you" (Ps. 63:8), we then say with David. "Herein is the call for patient endurances and faithfulness on the part of the saints" (Rev. 13:10). It is precisely in this that the steadfastness of Jacob and of the disciples on their way to Emmaus came out, namely, in that the former did not let the angel go and the latter did not let Christ go, even when they wanted to go. Thus, we read in 2 Chronicles 32:31 that God "left" Hezekiah the king to himself "to test him and to know everything that was in his heart." And in Deuteronomy 8:2, Moses gives the reason why God led the children of Israel to wander around for forty years in the wilderness. He says, "To humble you and to test you in order to know what was in your heart, whether or not you would keep his commands." And in Deuteronomy 13:3, we read, "The Lord your God is testing you to find out whether you love him with all your heart and with all your soul." Thus, God refines and tries the soul in "the furnace of affliction," as Isaiah puts it (48:10). His visitations are tests, which is also why the two words are frequently used simultaneously, as, for example, in Job 7:18: "You visit him every morning and test him every moment"; and in Psalm 17:3: "If you try my heart, if you visit me by night, if you test me, you will find no wickedness in me." It is a powerful proof of faithfulness and steadfastness, then, to be able to say with David, "Prove me, O Lord, and try me; test my heart and my mind" (Ps. 26:2), or with Isaiah, "I will wait for the Lord, who is hiding his face from the house of Jacob, and I will hope in him" (8:17).

This is different language from that which King Joram's messenger spoke when he said, "This trouble is from the Lord! Why should I wait for the Lord any longer?" (2 Kings 6:33).

Second, spiritual abandonment comes over us in order to effect in us a greater aversion, a stronger abhorrence, hatred, and mortification of sin. We so strongly feel its bitter aftertaste because now we have to forego all comfort and joy and, as it were, burn in a hell. "Woe is us that we have sinned so grievously," laments the soul and cries out with Job, "If I have sinned, what have I done to you, O watcher of men?" (v. 20). The soul cannot but prosecute with an everlasting hatred the evil it has done, on account of which so much evil has come upon it. God repeatedly testifies to this, and the soul also knows very well that, on account of sin, God turns his face away from us and that, on account of iniquity, the glory of God departs from the temple. "You have hidden your face from us and made us waste away because of our sins" (Isa. 64:7). And Jeremiah asks, "Consider then . . . how evil and bitter it is for you when you forsake the Lord your God" (Jer. 2:19).

Third, it occurs to deeply humble us, for, as we can see, there is no soul with so little self-esteem, no soul that so rejects and despises itself, as the abandoned soul. It dares not think itself a son but requests permission to be only a hireling; it dares not sit at the table of the Lord as a guest but wants to lie under it like a dog; it dares not touch him but only the fringe of his garment. That is how it is with the soul that was often very bold in the past when things went well with it and it was satiated with spiritual gifts of grace and tasted the feeling of it all. "Jeshurun grew fat and wicked; filled with food, he became heavy and sleek. He abandoned the God who made him and rejected the Rock his Savior" (Deut. 32:15). Augustine says, "The Bridegroom is coming to comfort you; he departs to admonish you so that too much consolation would not make you proud; so that, if the Bridegroom were always with you, you would not come to despise your companions and not therefore ascribe this constant visitation to grace but to nature." Sometimes this grace is withdrawn, not on account of the pride that is already present but on account of the pride that would come if it were not withdrawn. Paul gives us an example of that in 2 Corinthians 12:7 with reference to himself.

Fourth, it occurs the more to conform us in all respects to the image of his Son, for to that end we were predestined from eternity (Rom. 8:29; Phil. 3:10). Christ, the beloved of the Father, was also afflicted with these trials but very differently and much harder than we. They struck him so hard that we might be delivered by this means, not from knowing them somewhat but from knowing them as the punishment of our sins, and still bearing in them the sting of the curse. He was in more fearful trials, says Luke, although at that point he was not yet physically opposed by any human being; nevertheless, his mind was so deeply troubled—even to the point of death—that he did not know where to turn or to hide. He found no help from his disciples, no comfort from his Father. He was abandoned by heaven and earth. He had to empty a cup of hellish punishment. Though scarcely able to do it, he had to suffer the punishment of all our sins and drink the most accursed water of the curse. "My Father," he prayed accordingly, "if possible, take this cup from me," but he immediately added the words, "yet not my will but yours be done" (Luke 22:42). The apostle says of him, "During the days of Jesus' life on earth, he offered up prayers and petitions with loud cries and tears to the one who could save him from death, and he was heard for his godly fear" (Heb. 5:7). And Christ had earlier lamented, "Now my soul is troubled, and what shall I say? Father, save me from this hour? No, it was for this very reason I came to this hour" (John 12:27). And on the cross he cried out, "My God, my God, why have you forsaken me?" (Matt. 27:46). Forsaken by God, who was nevertheless still his God, and in such a way that God was nevertheless able to "forsake" him for such a time and in such a horrible way. It behooves us to be like the image of that Son so that, as he was willing to be like us in the sense that he was tempted like us in all things but without sin, now we would be conformed to him in the sense that we would not remain totally untempted in this respect.

Over and over it was precisely this conformity to Christ that was the reason for the holy martyrs to suffer all they had to suffer, and so it ought to be for us. When on the occasion of John Huss's execution his executioners put on him the white tabard, he said, "People also mocked my Lord Jesus Christ when they dressed him in a white garment and he was sent to Pilate by Herod." And when they put on his head a paper cap with painted devils on it, he said, "My Lord Jesus Christ, being innocent, eagerly wore for me, a miserable sinner, a sharper and much heavier crown of thorns to the place of his disgraceful death. Why should I, miserable sinner that I am, not very eagerly wear on my head this much lighter crown, though it is meant to insult and mock me?" His fellow brother, Jerome of Prague, when his executioners put such a hat on his head, similarly commented, "When my Lord Jesus Christ was about to die, he wore for me, a wretched human being, a much more painful crown of thorns on his head. With this hat, therefore, and in his honor, I am happy to walk into the fire." The Italian martyr Fanine, before he was burnt alive in 1550, spoke these words: "Dear brothers, I am not afraid and cheerfully accept the message of my death, for the sake of my Lord and Savior Jesus Christ, who did not spare his life to redeem me from death." Louis Marsac, a French nobleman, underwent the same lot in 1553. The words recorded of him are: "If we wish to live with Christ, it is also fair to suffer with him beforehand, for how would we look if we wanted to enjoy with Christ good things, honor, and glory and refused to share his cross?" Lawrence Saunders, professor of theology and a minister at the time of Queen Mary, was similarly burned to death on account of his faith (1555) in a forest at Coventry, England. "My Lord Jesus Christ," he said, "did not refuse, on my behalf, to drink a much more bitter and sorrowful drink; and should I not respond to that act, especially now that he summons and admonishes me to do this?" Francis Varlut, facing the stake, which he mounted in 1562 in the neighborhood of Doornik, consoled himself with these remarkable words:

> True, we must first go through the fire before we come to Christ; nevertheless, we know that we pass through death into life and from earth into heaven. If we are despised with Christ, we will also be exalted and glorified with him; if we suffer with him, we shall also reign with him; if we wear his crown of thorns, he will also share with us his crown of honor; if we allow ourselves to be taken with shame, for the whole world to see, to the place of punishment and let ourselves, as he did, be condemned and burned, we will also live with him in eternal joy and glory.

To say nothing about the praiseworthy and renowned deed of Duke Godfried of Bouillon, who, when Christians conquered Palestine in 1099 and he was to be crowned king at Jerusalem, refused the golden crown people wanted to put on his head. "It would not be fitting for a poor sinner as I am," he said, "to wear a golden crown, where the Savior of the whole world, the king of heaven, wore a crown of thorns, sprinkled with his precious blood." Godfried, accordingly, had a crown of thorns put on his head as well. This is all we will report about this story.

Fifth, God visits us with these trials to kindle in us the more vigorously the valuation of his grace. No good is ever valued more highly than when it is lacking or desired. As long as people have the enjoyment of it, the value of it is discounted or forgotten. We see this, remember, with the people of Israel in the wilderness. They remembered and hankered for the fleshpots of Egypt and lamented, "Now our strength has dried up, and there is nothing at all but this manna to look at" (Num. 11:6). There is the well-known saying, "Familiarity breeds contempt." Augustine wrote, "The Bridegroom goes away in order not, by being always with her, to be despised, but to be found again with all the more joy inasmuch as he has been sought longer." Joab refused to come although Absalom had twice sent for him, but when the latter set fire to his field, he came immediately (2 Sam. 14:30–31).

Now, this valuation of God's grace is manifested in three ways: (1) when it is lacking and is sought for all the more diligently; (2) when it returns and is welcomed all the more heartily; (3) when it is present and is preserved all the more carefully. "For this reason he possibly withdrew from us," says Bernard of Christ in discussing the Song of Solomon, "that he would be the more zealously called back and the more firmly held on to." And in Psalm 77, Asaph declares, "In the day of my trouble I sought the LORD; in the night my hand was stretched out without let-up" (v. 2); while the bride in the Song of Solomon cries out upon Christ's return, "I found him whom my soul loves. I held him and would not let him go" (3:4).

2

In the first section, we discussed illness and spiritual anxiety. Now we will focus attention on the following two points: First, how the soul must conduct itself in this situation; here we need to bring comfort. Next, how the soul can be delivered from that condition; here we need aids against this evil in order to be finally saved and delivered from it. We will treat both points in succession—the first we will discuss in this chapter, the second in the next one.

We now imagine ourselves to be speaking with such a defeated soul about its illness and to comfort it as vividly and as powerfully as we are able. "Comfort," Paul calls to the Thessalonians in his first letter (5:14), "comfort the feebleminded, support the weak," and in the opening of Isaiah 40, God says, "Comfort ye, comfort ye my people. Speak ye comfortably to Jerusalem."

What is really meant here is "to speak to the heart." To speak to someone's heart means to speak to him as he desires in his situation, that is, so that it makes an impression on him, that it helps him, and that it is for his well-being. That's what we read about Shechem in relation to Dinah, Jacob's daughter: "And he loved the damsel, and he spoke to the heart of the damsel" (Gen. 34:3). Judges 19:3 says that the Levite arose and went after his wife "to speak to her heart and bring her back." And we hear Ruth say to Boaz, "Let me find favor in your sight, my lord, for you have comforted me, because you have spoken to the heart of your handmaid" (Ruth

2:13). All these places therefore show that "to comfort" means in effect "to speak to someone's heart."

We will now therefore speak to the heart of this spiritually abandoned person, and in doing so we have as a goal four items: First, we want, as much as we are able, to soften and decrease his evil. From Job's saying, "My bed shall comfort me, my couch shall ease my complaints" (7:13), it appears that comfort is the decreasing of evil.

Second, we want to strengthen the heart and give good courage. Here we want to point to the sayings of Jesus to his disciples: "In the world ye shall have tribulation, but be of good cheer" (John 16:33). "Fear not." The word of the Lord to Isaiah: "Take heed, and be quiet; fear not, neither be fainthearted" (Isa. 7:4). The word of Moses to the people: "Fear not. Remain firm and see the salvation of the Lord" (Exod. 14:13). The word of Christ in John 14:27: "Let not your heart be troubled, neither let it be afraid." The word of Paul to the congregation of Thessalonica: "May the Lord Jesus Christ himself comfort your hearts and strengthen you" (2 Thess. 2:17). From these sayings it is sufficiently clear that comfort serves to strengthen the heart.

Third, we must, if possible, take away the evil. We read in Isaiah 51:11, "Sorrow and mourning shall flee away."

Fourth, in place of the earlier sadness, we must bring joy and spiritual gladness. We read in Jeremiah 31:13, "I will turn their mourning into joy and will comfort them and make them rejoice from their sorrow. Isaiah 66:10, 13–14 says, "Rejoice with Jerusalem, and be glad with her, all you that love her; rejoice for joy with her, all you that mourn for her. . . . As one whom his mother comforts, so will I comfort you; and you shall be comforted in Jerusalem. When you see this, your heart will rejoice, and your bones will flourish like an herb." "Fear not," said the angel of the Lord to the shepherds, "for behold, I bring you great joy" (Luke 2:10). That's how true comfort works; it takes away the evil in order to bring in the good, and, having stilled the sadness, it gives joy (cf. Rom. 5:3; 2 Cor. 7:4–5).

This requires a special and holy learning. Isaiah says, "The Lord God hath given me the tongue of the learned that I should know how to speak a word in season to him that is weary" (50:4), and David lauds as blessed "he who conducts himself wisely toward the afflicted" (Ps. 22:24). Someone has said very truly, "No more than the same medicines can serve all bodies is the same speech suitable for every soul."

Now we proceed to the issue itself and come to the patient. However, before we say wherewith he may comfort himself and from which veins he can draw God's comfort, we will lay before him two things as a basis for our address and as proofs.

First, that he is in the state of God's grace and that he is a child of God. There are sufficient evidences and proofs of this state present in him, also in the midst of this misery, even though he does not notice it. We therefore show this to him and let him feel it tangibly. Before this we determine that we are dealing with someone who experiences such abandonments as we have discussed above, that is, a righteous and God-fearing soul. In the second place, we must prove that along with these abandonments and trials the grace of God is possible; this grace does not succumb but (although often not seen) continues to persevere eternally for the soul.

About the first item, pay heed to whatever in you proves that you belong to God, that you share in God's grace, that you are a child of God, and that God's Spirit is in you, for these things do not occur in the reprobate and damned, who are estranged from God and Christ. Pay heed, then, first of all to your sins that grieve and oppress you, over which you lament and against which you struggle. And then tell me, what is the state of your heart? Is it not true that you feel that the sins are a burden, indeed a heavy burden? Do you not shudder under their weight, do they not lead you to sincere sadness, and do you not have remorse for all your sins? Do you not desire sincerely that you had never committed these sins? If this is so, it is well with you!

You can be assured that, since such feelings about sin do not occur in an unconverted person, you, brought to this place through God's Spirit, are converted and therefore share in the saving grace of God. After all, you cannot possess these feelings from yourself. As the prophet Zechariah says in chapter 12, it is "through the grace of the Spirit" (v. 10). Read also Psalm 51:17: "The sacrifices of God are a broken spirit; a broken and a contrite heart—these, O God, you will not despise." And note Isaiah 66:1–2: "The Lord says, 'Heaven is my throne, and earth is my footstool. Where is the house that you will build me? And where is the place of my rest? For all those things my hand has made, and all those things have been,' says the LORD. 'But I will look on this person—the one who is poor and of a contrite spirit and who trembles at my word.'"

Our Lord has chosen two places for himself—one for his glory in heaven and one for his grace in the contrite heart. He sees and lives in the most humble and the most contrite person. Whoever grants the Lord a place in his heart, God gives a place in heaven afterward. He says, "Come to me all who are weary and burdened, and I will give you rest" (Matt. 11:28; see also Isa. 55:1; 57:15; 1 Samuel 1; Acts 2).

Second, it is a certain sign of grace in you that you esteem grace as highly as you do. Just think—do you possess anything that is more precious and beloved by you, that you work harder for, that you regard higher, than the gracious favor of God and the experience of that favor?

What do you think, did the flesh or the world teach you to value the grace of God so highly—higher than the world or than yourself? Or did the Spirit of God and his special grace in you teach you that? Yes, indeed! The fact that we value God so highly is *always* caused by God working in us, and this evaluation is possessed only by him who (as the apostle Peter says) shares in the divine nature, that is, divine grace and likeness. Paul could never have written in his letter to the Philippians, "I indeed count all things as a loss for the excellence of the knowledge of Christ Jesus my Lord, for whom I have suffered the loss of all things and count them as rubbish, that I may gain Christ" (3:8) if the grace of God had not worked this in him and had not qualified him for that. He writes in the same way to the people in Colosse: "Thanking God the Father, who has qualified us" (Col. 1:12). To leave everything in order to enjoy God! To be able to say, "If I have only the Lord, then I desire nothing else," or to exclaim with the bride in the Song of Solomon, "If someone gave all the possessions in his house for this love, he would be despised" (8:7). Whoever is able to say these things is unspeakably rich! Is there anyone who can speak or act in this way without sharing in the grace of God?

No! We say with Augustine, "Whatever is next to God is too small." Or think of the holy martyr John Diasius. His brother Alphonsus (who later murdered him in an atrocious way) offered John five hundred ducats—which he took from the church's possessions in Rome every year—if John would go with him and change his religion. John answered:

> Brother, I am not as avaricious as you possibly think. If I had sought money or goods, I would have conducted my affairs differently. The little knowledge of divine truth, which the Lord has graciously given me—that I consider my highest honor. And I count my good conscience higher and of more value than all the money and all the goods of the world.

Third, the fact that you have such a heartfelt, complete, unsatisfied desire, craving, and longing for God's grace is certain proof of that grace in you. There could not be such desire without grace. On the contrary, it is certain proof of grace. I say "craving," but it must be a *sincere* craving. And note well that I do not say "feeling" that one *has* grace. No, a *genuine craving* to have this grace is a certain proof that one already possesses the grace. Scripture teaches us that it is a proof that we have that grace, not only when we *taste* and, as it were, *eat* God's goodness but also when we *hunger* and *thirst* after it. Christ the Savior, who alone saves those who will ever be saved, himself says in Matthew 5, "Blessed are those who hunger and thirst after righteousness, for they shall be filled" (v. 6). As you notice, he does not say "the righteous"; no, he already counts blessed "those who hunger and thirst after righteousness."

Just as Nehemiah, in his prayer, calls "God's servants" those who have a desire to serve God. In Nehemiah 1:11 he prays, "O LORD, let your ear be attentive to the prayer of your servant and to your servants who desire to fear your name." Indeed, all serving of God, even of the most holy, does not consist so much in deeds as in inclination and desires. Jerome says, with reference to himself, "I have not so much refrained a little from sin as I have begun to want to refrain."

God's Holy Word shows so abundantly and powerfully that the gracious address and comfort often comes to those who are miserable beggars, who bring nothing but sheer emptiness. But they hunger and thirst and have nothing but empty hands. Those are the ones whom God actually wants, since he does not need us or what we have. After all, our goodness does not touch him. Mary says in her song, "He has filled the hungry with good things, and the rich he has sent away empty" (Luke 1:53). And in Isaiah 55:1, the invitation says, "All you who are thirsty, come to the waters, and you who have no money, come, buy, and eat. Yes, come, buy wine and milk without money and without price." Who is invited here? Not the satisfied or rich but the thirsty ones, and that is precisely your soul. It is thirsty. To what is it invited? To fill its want; to share in and enjoy the milk and wine of God's abundant and rich grace. He does not sell his grace; he grants it as a gift, for nothing. After all, he *gives* his bread to the hungry. That is what a righteous person does, and that is, in the first place, what *the Lord God* does.

Do you not desire to reach out for that? Is this not the only thing that you seek? And how could you achieve that if you needed money or goods or work for it—efforts that first had to please God and on account of which he would then grant his grace? If that were so, then you would never share in this grace, because you possess nothing. But just at that point when you say, "I do not have any money," then comes the loving invitation: "You who have no money, come, buy *without* money and *without* price." And in the next verse, those are actually punished who "weigh out money for that which is not bread, and their labor for that which does not satisfy." In John 7:37, we read, "And on the last day, the great day of the feast, Jesus stood and cried out, 'If anyone is thirsty, let him come to me and drink.'" So as you notice, Jesus especially desires thirsty souls, and he promises his grace to them. In Jeremiah 50:4–5, we read, "'In those days, and in that time,' says the Lord, 'the children of Israel will come, they and the children of Judah together, going and weeping. They will go and seek the Lord their God. They will ask the way to Zion and turn their faces toward it. They will come and be added to the Lord in an eternal covenant that will not be forgotten.'"

If perhaps someone might want to find an escape by saying, "That's well and good for those who come, but not for me, because I'm not coming," then I say, "You're not coming? You don't want to come? Wouldn't you want to come not just with all your might but actually running to him, even flying to him, that you, as it were, did not stop running to the Lord?" Well, it's actually that kind of desire that we are talking about here. And we note that just as such a desire in a person's heart is certain proof of God's grace, just as certain will all these promises come to and belong to him. It's just as Augustine says, "To long for the help of grace is already a beginning of grace." And speaking about catechizing the unlearned he says,

"Often God's mercy comes through the service of the catechism teachers so that a person, brought under the influence, now wants to become what he formerly had imagined; and when he *begins to want* we must assume that it is already there."

Earlier, Basil said, "Just want to, and God will come of his own accord." And the same church father supports this saying as follows: After having pointed to the inclination that caused the father to walk toward and embrace the prodigal son upon his return, Basil says that "he (the son) *began* to speak, and then the Father embraces him. When you then also notice and observe how the Father is moved with mercy, then you will not cut off hope for your forgiveness." In another place, Basil says, "If the will is prepared, then there is nothing further that can hinder." And Jerome spoke as follows: "The total will to do something is counted as the deed."

Studying the sayings in Holy Scripture, we see that the Lord Jesus considers the *will* to do evil as if *the deed itself* were committed. We read in Matthew 5:28, "But I say to you, whoever looks at a woman to lust for her has already committed adultery with her in his heart," and 1 John 3:15 says, "Whoever hates his brother is a murderer." While this is said in relation to the will toward evil, we must also consider the other side: that it is true with relation to the good will, which God also takes for the deed itself. That is why Paul, in his second letter to the congregation in Corinth, could write, "A person is acceptable according to what he has, not according to what he does not have" (2 Cor. 8:12). Paul wants to say that if someone lacks the deed, he is still acceptable if he only shows that he has the will to do it. Bernard says, "With a good will nobody can be lost." It is therefore the unanimous opinion of all theologians that in this situation the will must be considered the deed.

In his *Consultation,* Georg Cassandra says that if one asks a penitent about his grief and finds that his grief is not sufficient, then one must ask the penitent whether he does not *wish* that he were more grieved and whether he does not sorrow that his grief is not greater. In the same way, we also ask the soul that laments that it *cannot* believe, love, trust, and so on, "Do you *wish* that you could do all of that?" And if such wishing and desiring is honest and true and is coupled with a diligent striving to obtain the desired operation of grace and salvation, then such desiring is a good and certain sign. For that reason, we therefore suspend our judgment even about that well-known and unfortunate Italian lawyer Franciscus Spira, born in Citadella. The history of this man, who was about fifty years old and had a wife and eleven children, is known from several letters written in Latin and printed in Basel in 1550 and later translated into German, English, Dutch, and French (1644).

This Spira, driven by temporal concerns (the retaining of honor and possessions), against all admonition and warning of his conscience, renounced his faith in Venice in the year 1548 to the papal legate John Casa. After this, Spira was so distressed in his soul that he had to wrestle with the most terrible trials. Because of these trials, which are seldom encountered in such degree by any other person, he became a pitiable example of apostasy and abandonment to the whole world. After he had denied the truth in Venice and persisted in that after his return to the city where he lived, God gripped him in his conscience, and from that hour until the end of his life, his poor soul was most severely distressed and anguished, in the most lamentable manner, by all kinds of trials.

How people in that time judged him can be seen from the testimony of Paul Vergerius, bishop of Justinopolis, who had rented a house in Padua. Spira had also been brought here, and Vergerius's house was close to Spira's so that he usually was with Vergerius. In his *Apologia,* Vergerius testifies that Franciscus lived without hope. He did want to return to God but thought that he could not do so. We silently pass by the judgment that others have pronounced. On the basis of his burning desire and his heartfelt longing for God and his grace (longing that he frequently displayed), we consider ourselves duty-bound to suspend our judgment—if not to speak in his favor.

He frequently gave expression to that heartfelt longing, as when he sighed, "Oh, that I, if only for a moment, might feel God's love in me to the same extent that I now feel him to be my bitter enemy." Or, "This is how it is—I cannot believe you people or entrust myself to God's grace. I wish that I could do it, and therefore I can say that I do not wish it completely. I would wish that I could entrust myself to God, but I cannot, and therefore I cannot say, 'I wish.'" On another occasion he said, "I tell you again, if I could only feel and experience one drop of God's grace, that God was reconciled to me (the least evidence would be sufficient), then I would not refuse to undergo a thousand and more years of hellish punishment."

At the insistence of Vergerius, Franciscus proceeded to pray. Already with the first words, "Our Father who art in heaven," he burst into tears so that he had to stop. When the bystanders pointed out that this was a good sign, he answered, "I lament my misery, because I see that I have been abandoned by God and I cannot call upon him as ardently as I used to do." At Vergerius's request, he continued to pray, and when he came to the words "Thy kingdom come," he said, "O Lord, bring me also into this kingdom; I pray to you, do not shut me out." And when he had spoken the fourth petition, "Give us our daily bread," he added, "O Lord, I have sufficient abundance to feed this body, but there is another bread. I humbly pray for this bread of your grace, for I know that without this bread I am a dead person." And to the petition "Lead us not into temptation," he added, "I have been brought into temptation. Be my help so that I may be delivered from it. My enemy has conquered me, and I pray to you, help me, so that I may conquer him."

According to history, he said all this with such a sad voice, and his tears that streamed down expressed so completely what was in his heart, that the hearts of all those who were present were filled with sadness and pity. When Spira had finished his prayer, Vergerius said, "Praise to God, Franciscus, you sigh and you pray with a heartfelt longing to find grace, and that is certainly proof that you are not completely rejected." Spira answered, "That faith and that trust are gifts of God, and that is precisely what I am lacking; I cannot hope or trust God's grace and mercy toward me. Oh! If God would only give me one thing—that I would have hope in my forgiveness and could believe therein."

Another author tells about Spira and that he said, "Oh, that my state were righteous! If I, through the favor of divine providence, were restored to the state of grace, then I would scorn the threats of tyrants, bear all torments with a great and unconquerable spirit, and gladly convey Christ in my mouth, eye, and heart, until the flames took away my spirit and my body was reduced to dust and ashes."

The same author also relates in his letter that Spira passed an adverse judgment on a certain book written twenty-one years earlier by a philosopher named Peretus, who maintained that the miracles performed by Jesus can be explained by natural causes in natural ways. In response, Spira said, "The natural man does not understand the things which are of God's Spirit."

There were also those who based their judgment on that which Spira formerly experienced in his heart. Spira therefore testified in reference to his earlier state, "I knew God as my Father, not only because of creation but also because of regeneration. I knew him through his Son, our Savior. I was able to call on him and dared to hope for the forgiveness of sins. I felt his sweetness, peace, and comfort in my heart."

At the time, Spira considered all of that hypocrisy, for he knew that a true believer and a genuine convert cannot completely fall away. However, with a sick person we do not base our judgment so much on what he says as on what we observe in him. In the same way, we pass judgment on a soul more on the basis of appearances that we observe than on the words of a frightened judgment that, in reference to itself, is often totally wrong. It is therefore on the basis of these evidences, sighs, and appearances that we saw in Spira that we do not dare to pass light or adverse judgment on him, although one cannot deny that he was a frightening example and frequently showed himself as a despairing and condemned person.

Still, the reading of his history is very useful and edifying for people who have a rash and easy view of life and who consider the truth lightly. Bishop Paul Vergerius, a conscientious man, testifies that this very history was the cause of his conversion. Summoned by the pope, he was at the point of going to Rome in order to become more closely tied to the pope and his domain when he became acquainted with Spira. As a result, he preferred to forsake his goods and friends, fatherland and bishopric, yes, everything. He then went to Basel, and, arriving at Dr. Borrhaus's home, he said, "Oh, Borrhaus, I never would have come to Basel if I had not met Spira." And just because he had testified to the truth of Spira's history so ardently, he felt himself compelled to write an "apologia" and let it be distributed so that others would be admonished through it.

Fourth, this story is proof of divine grace in the soul, that it hates and shuns sin—yes, all sins, even the most dear, deeply rooted sin. The fact that you are so averse to sin, and that you warn everyone against sin, and that you avoid and refrain from it—is that not by God's grace working in you? Certainly, this is better—better than if you were eagerly chasing sin and giving yourself to it without any second thoughts. But why then would you now deny that God's grace has been working in you, the grace of repentance, which is a part of this, for "what is born of the flesh is flesh, but what is born of the Spirit is spirit" (John 3:6).

Since you now know that nothing comes from the flesh (in which, to quote Paul, "no good lives") except that which is fleshly, you must also admit that there is nothing spiritual, or nothing that is against the flesh, unless it comes from the Holy Spirit. "The firm foundation of God stands, having this seal: The Lord knows those who are his, and everyone who names the name of Christ departs from unrighteousness" (2 Tim. 2:19). Departing from unrighteousness is an attribute and sign of him who belongs to Christ, to God, and is thus, as it were, firmly sealed by God. (See also Ezek. 18:5–10.)

Fifth, one can discern in this soul an earnest attempt, a great desire for, and a diligent practice of many Christian virtues, and all such with great circumspection.

You see and feel yourself compelled to good works, and, as much as in you lies, you want to abide by all God's commandments. You strive to love God and your neighbor with your whole heart. And now that you are in this spiritual state, you try, more than ever, to walk carefully. All this must convince you that God's grace is in you and that these trials are beneficial and useful for your godly walk and that they strengthen you therein. Christ says, "Without me you can do nothing" (John 15:5). And in his first letter to God's congregation in Corinth, Paul writes, "No one can say that Jesus is Lord, except by the Holy Spirit" (12:3). "Or do you not know that your body is a temple of the Holy Spirit, who is in you, whom you have from God, and you are not your own?" (6:19). We must therefore confess with Paul that we of ourselves are not able to think anything from ourselves but that our ability comes from God, who works in us both to will and to do his good pleasure. Since now, in this regard, you strongly feel God's Spirit and grace in you so that you are compelled to all good works, why do you then still doubt his presence?

Let us now concentrate your attention especially on one point. In your deepest heart, you feel a strong love for your fellow believers in Christ, for the brothers and for the saints whom you greatly esteem and love, and that not for some temporal reasons but only because of their godliness and their gifts. Then I ask you, how could you esteem and love these brothers for their godliness if it were not that God had created that same spirit of holiness in you—the spirit that binds all together into one body? In your heart, you highly value the holiness and devotion of the pious, as well as their state of grace. This appreciation comes from the same principle, rests on the same foundation, has the same cause, as the Spirit who creates the desire and striving for holiness in you. You highly honor and praise others, and you say with David, "All my delight is in the saints who are on the earth, and in the excellent ones" (Ps. 16:3). You know and speak highly of the saints as the most excellent. Does all this not prove that you share in the same spirit with them and are driven with them toward the same goal? We see that a person who is happily engaged in learning always finds his pleasure in enlarging his knowledge. In the same way, it can be no different when we see the person whose heart goes out to the godly and pious for no other reason than their godliness, that he, driven by the same spirit of holiness and piety, will highly esteem them. Is it for this reason, then, that the ungodly do not love the pious because of their piety? On the contrary, they hate them. But the opposite is equally true: To love the pious and their piety is a sign of a pious heart. John says in his first letter, "We know that we have passed from death to life when we love the brothers. He who loves his brother remains in the light" (3:14). And Jesus says, "By this all will know that you are my disciples, if you have love for each other" (John 13:35). In these souls, one sees clearly that their inclination reaches out mightily to the pious and to the church, that they strongly desire their prosperity and rejoice if it goes well with them, saying, "Oh Jerusalem, if I forget you, may I forget my right hand" (Ps. 137:5). This is a good and certain sign that they belong to the church and among those pious whose well-being they heartily desire. Scripture says, "Pray for the peace of Jerusalem. It will go well with those who love you" (Ps. 122:6).

These five manifestations that we successively considered are always present in the soul and can be observed in the soul amid the most violent trials. The first manifestation looks at remorse, the next two at faith, the last two at conversion. We presented to the soul proof, on the basis of these five manifestations, that the saving grace of God was present. And this is especially what we intended: to show where God was in relation to the soul. "O Zion, Messenger of good news, climb to a high mountain. O Jerusalem, shout to Zion from the mountaintops! Shout louder to Jerusalem—do not be afraid. Tell the towns of Judah, 'Your God is coming!'" (Isa. 40:9).

If someone objects, "But in me all of that is so incomplete, so feeble, and stained with so many sins," then I give this answer: That is certainly true, and God therefore does not prescribe a certain measure; he does not outline the steps; he does not say that the remorse, the faith, the conversion must be of such and such degree. No, he requires nothing but the desire itself—but such desire must be absolute and in uprightness of heart. And this is precisely the best proof of uprightness, that a person laments his shortcomings, recognizes his imperfection, just as His Excellency Prince Maurits said on his deathbed, "There is nothing in the world that troubles me. The only thing that grieves me is that the remorse over my sins is not as great as it should be, and therefore I lament that I cannot improve myself and serve God as I desired." Indeed, wonderful words, which are certain proof of a converted, heavenly soul! For this is precisely our perfection, that we know our imperfection and lament our sins, especially that we lament that we cannot lament our sins *more*. It is told of the martyr William Gardiner (1552) that, continually weeping about his great weakness, he lamented "that he could not hate his sins enough, and that he could not love true godliness diligently enough."

In the second place, we had resolved to prove to such a soul that *simultaneously* with these spiritual abandonments the grace of God, faith, and salvation can also be present. In other words, we must prove that (1) faith and God's grace in the soul, (2) God's gracious favor, (3) or salvation are not destroyed in or because of these trials. In other words, we must prove the perseverance of the saints.

That neither faith nor God's grace in the soul can be destroyed is shown in 1 John 3:9: "for his seed remains in him"; in John 14:17: "the Spirit of truth remains in you and you know him"; in verse 16: "He will send another Comforter who will abide with you into eternity"; in John 4:13–14: "Whoever drinks of this water will thirst again, but whoever drinks of the water that I give him will never thirst; the water that I give him will become a fountain of water, springing up into everlasting life"; and in Philippians 1:6: "Being confident of this, that he who has begun a good work in you will complete it until the day of Jesus Christ."

Neither is God's gracious favor destroyed. Paul says in 1 Corinthians 1:8, "God will confirm you to the end, that you may be blameless in the day of our Lord Jesus Christ," and he points out in verse 9 "that God is faithful." The apostle Peter declares that "we are kept by the power of God through faith for salvation, ready to be revealed in the last time" (1 Peter 1:5). And David testifies in Psalm 37, "Though the righteous fall, he shall not be cast away, for the Lord upholds his hand" (v. 24). (See also Jer. 32:39–40.)

As proof that salvation cannot be destroyed either, we point to John 6:39–40. There we read, "This is the will of the Father who sent me, that of all he has given me I should lose nothing, but should raise it up at the last day. And this is the will of him who sent me, that everyone who sees the Son and believes in him may have everlasting life; and I will raise him up at the last day." (See also John 10:28–30; Rom. 8:29ff.) Yes, according to Matthew 16:18, the gates of hell can do nothing.

We have now shown that righteous believers and those who have once shared in the saving grace of God, through God's power and the faithfulness of our Savior, will always remain secure in that faith and cannot completely fall from that grace so that they cannot change from a child of God into a child of the devil. We have nearly provided proof for the abandoned soul that its state cannot become such that it would be rejected by God or could completely fall from grace. A person who is a child of God cannot become a child of the devil.

We have also nearly provided proof to the beleaguered soul that it cannot attain such a state that it would be rejected by God or could completely fall from grace. After all, earlier it also shared in God's grace and bore the certain evidences of such grace. Add to that the perseverance of God's love of his saints and the perseverance of the saints in his love, and it is impossible that these two could ever be broken or separated. We must also note the fact that the beleaguered soul does not have a righteous and strong desire for grace *now* but truly enjoyed this grace *earlier*. The soul can draw strong comfort from this knowledge: Whatever happens, even if heaven and earth were moved, yes, even if the terrors of hell sneered at this one soul, yet it would be kept and would surely remain God's possession, even if it went through the valley of the shadow of death. That is why those who wanted to comfort Franciscus Spira pointed so emphatically to his earlier life in order to demonstrate from it his faith and conversion. When they had done so, they could confidently proceed and pass judgment on the present as well as the future, and they could, finally, build their comfort on the foundation they had laid.

According to the communication of Johannes Bogerman to Prince Maurice,[1] a beleaguered minister was healed in this manner: Someone asked the minister whether he did not remember how in earlier times he had frequently experienced comfort and joy in God's grace in his soul. "Well," he continued to comfort the minister, "in view of what you experienced earlier, you can calmly go into the future, because what you are now going through is only a black cloud and the hour of trial. And since God never regrets that he granted his grace to us, you will soon again have what you desire so heartily." And that is what happened. Especially with this trial, the remembrance of the earlier condition must provide comfort for the situation that one is going through now. Asaph also experienced this, and therefore he can say in Psalm 77, "I remember the days of old" (v. 5).

You notice how true and comforting the doctrine of the perseverance of the saints is, and why the devil rages so violently against this doctrine and fights against it through the mouth of all heretics and erring spirits, and you see the same with the doctrine of grace. Man in his natural depravity is not able of himself and through his own strength to bring forth true and spiritual goodness. (See Rom. 7:17; 8:7; 2 Cor. 3:5; Eph. 2:1–2.)

All this comes into being through God's grace, and such good stirrings, impulses, desires, and attempts are therefore the certain operations and proofs of God's grace. And just as all operations are indications of the presence of the operating cause, so these operations and proofs let us know the presence of the grace of God. If, however, one assumes that this can happen through man's own will and power or that one can lose these operations of grace completely, then there remains no certain proof that these impulses are signs of God's grace or that man will always remain in this grace that he once had. Both errors would be in conflict with the foundation of

1. Johannes Bogerman and Maurice of Orange were prominent Dutch leaders in the seventeenth century.

all salutary comfort and with the proof of divine Scripture, as well as with what the Christian church has always taught.

Durandus, a scholastic papist, discussing the question as to whether man can sufficiently satisfy for his sin, said:

> The idea that best agrees with godliness of the faith is that we assign the *least* to ourselves and the *most* to God so that every pious person can say with the psalmist, "*He* has saved me because it pleased him," or with Paul, "It is not of him who wills, nor of the one who runs, but of God who shows mercy." And someone else says, "Dearest Jesus! I cannot desire anything good, even less do it, unless your grace inspires this desire or doing. Therefore, inspire me; bid me to do it; extol it to me; and then grant me the will and the strength to complete it."

We now turn to the discussion of the comforts themselves. Paying attention to the sources from which these comforts flow, we note that these are either general, if they apply to all troubles, or special, if they apply only to trials. These comforts flow from three sources:

1. from the nature and purpose of these spiritual trials
2. from God, as he reveals himself to these tried persons
3. from the grace of the gospel toward and about these tried persons

1. Regarding the first major point, that is, the burden of these spiritual trials, we note first of all that every person on earth must bear a cross. The one has this, another that, but no one is without. The proverb therefore says, "Every house has its cross." And if it pleases God to give you a cross, then, with Micah, bow yourself before the exalted Lord, accept it from his hand rather than follow your own desire or reject it for something else. Also, pay attention, both with respect to sin as well as help against sin, to the general necessity of burdens. After all, no person, not even a pious person, is exempt from burdens. Jesus himself said, "The cup that my Father has given me, shall I not drink from it?" (John 18:11). "Whoever wants to follow me must deny himself and take up his cross daily and follow me" (Matt. 16:24).

Second, no matter how great and heavy you feel your trial and abandonment may be, it is not a complete, total abandonment from God. It is not an abandonment of all grace but only of the *feeling* of grace. You do not *feel* the grace, as you would want. But really, is that so serious, to somewhat miss this feeling, while you keep the greatest, the deed itself? You do not really lose God, even though it is true that you lose the feeling of his grace. After all, even though you do not feel your stomach and your heart, don't you still have them?

What do you think, can that feeling not become somewhat shocked, darkened, and burdened? And have you not deserved what you are suffering? Just think how frequently that feeling capitulated to sin; yes, even though it was chastised, it capitulated. Think about Christ! Consider (although he did not deserve this) that the feeling of his Father's grace was beclouded and burdened completely for you!

Since this suffering now concerns only the *feeling* of grace, and you have kept what is of greatest weight and all that counts for your salvation, can you not be satisfied and comforted? Since God left you so much, and especially that which is of greatest weight, should you be ungrateful when you miss only that which is of less importance? God *cannot* completely leave you, and he shall not and will not do so, as is clear from what we have already said as proof of your state in grace and what you enjoy and feel in addition. Speaking about the church, Phillipe du Plessis-Mornay says somewhere, "Who could observe the fine thread of grace with which the soul is connected to God, the Lord!" This is firm and is proven sufficiently. God never leaves your soul *completely*, even though it may appear that he, for a time, hides his face, and you do not experience the feeling of his loving favor. Truly, the Lord does not forsake his beloved; they are kept into eternity.

Just hear what the Lord himself says: "'In a little wrath I hid my face from you for a moment, but with everlasting kindness will I have mercy on you,' says the LORD your Redeemer. 'For this is as the waters of Noah to me, when I swore that the waters of Noah should no more go over the earth; so have I sworn that I would not be angry with you or rebuke you. For the mountains shall depart and the hills be removed, but my kindness will not depart from you, neither shall the covenant of my peace be removed,' says the LORD, who has mercy on you" (Isa. 54:8–10; cf. Pss. 2:4; 118:18; Jer. 46:28; Lam. 3:33).

Third, these trials come only to God's children. Other burdens are general—the same happens to the righteous and the ungodly. But this cross is sanctified only for the pious, for God's beloved; other people do not know this cross; it is foreign to them. One can therefore not judge about the state of the soul on the basis of burdens that one has in common with other people; one can do that only on the basis of the abandonment that one does not have in common with others. And since no one is punished or chastised unless he has committed sin, and since no one can be God's child unless he is chastised, and since no one is chastised with this rod except the child of God, it follows that in the first case one decides from the person to the burden, but in the second case one decides from the burden to the person. Precisely because a person experiences this, one judges that his state is good.

Fourth, God's people have these trials in common. They do not touch you alone, with others being passed by; no, they come to *everyone.* It is true that they touch the one more and the other less, but since they are not sent to anyone except for the purpose of salvation, they bring greater fruit of salvation to those who are more heavily burdened. Think about the most saintly—above whom you may not place yourself (and you do not want to). Think about Christ, our Lord. How did he bear these trials and abandonments? How much did the Son of God, who could not be abandoned completely, suffer? Truly, everything. And would you now want to be an exception above all these? Certainly not, for do you not consider yourself blessed in their company?

Augustine says, "The Master of medicine has first drunk from the bitter cup himself, so that the sick would not hesitate to drink from it." We have already spoken about Christ's trials. We know that it was said of him, "In all things he was like we are; he was tempted but without sin" (Heb. 4:15). Hence, all those who want to live a godly life in Christ have to expect such oppressions. "Who of the saints," Jerome asks, "has been crowned without battle?" Thomas à Kempis declares, "I have never known a godly person who did not at times have this removal of grace." And Otto Casmannus says, "No one becomes saved who is not trained in this battle, before or in death." All this was not foreign to the saints of the

Bible either. Listen to Job in chapters 6 and 7; to David in Psalms 13, 32, 38, 39, 42; to Asaph in Psalm 77; and to Heman in Psalm 88. The man of God Luther, enabled by God, was used daily for the great work of the reformation of God's church, and he felt the abandonment of spirit. Both he and others testified to this. Casmannus says about Luther, "In 1527, the holy man Luther felt the heat of these trials so strongly that he, ill in body and soul from them, lay in bed, and later he himself testified that he would rather be imprisoned in the darkest dungeon his whole life than endure that pain again for one hour." One can name several martyrs who were similarly attacked, often just before their death. Someone therefore said, not without good reason, "Let this be a sign to you to know that when you are advancing on the road to the city of the King and are coming closer, that you will undergo the greatest temptations; the further you go, the greater the temptations. Because God does not give great gifts without great temptations."

Thomas Bilney, a martyr in England, on the night before he was burned at the stake, held his finger in a burning candle to test whether he could endure the pain of the fire. He had previously denied the truth, but later he experienced such trials, sadness, and abandonment that nothing could comfort him, and it appeared as if everything was against him. This lasted more than a year, because he fell from grace in 1529 and was not burned until 1531. Hugh Latimer, who was brought from popery to the truth by Bilney, testified of Bilney in a sermon before King Edward:

> I know a man, Bilney, little Bilney, that blessed martyr of God, who, at the time that he fell from grace, had such a conflict that his friends were concerned about leaving him by himself. They were with him night and day, comforting him, but no comfort could take root. And his heart was insensitive to the comforting Scripture passages that they applied to him; it was as if his heart was pierced with a sword. Nevertheless, after this he was awakened, and he bore his death with patience, dying against the tyrannical seat of Rome.

In another sermon, Latimer says:

> When Master Bilney was counseled by his friends to recant, he spent a whole year in such conflict and fear that nothing could divert him—not food, or drink, or any teaching from God's Word, because he

> thought that all of Scripture was against him and pointed to his damnation. I visited him often, but everything that one intended to convey to him for his comfort Bilney regarded as against him. However, after all this, everything worked out well, and God granted him such a strong and firm faith that he not only gave a testimony of his faith in the gospel of our Savior, Jesus Christ, but also let his body be burned for that same gospel that we now preach in England.

Another example is Robert Glover, an English nobleman, martyred in the year 1555. John Foxe tells about him from the account of the preacher Augustine Bernher, a friend of Glover:

> After Master Glover had been condemned to death by the bishop and was on the point of leaving this world, two or three days before his death, his heart became totally numb and abandoned from all spiritual comfort. In himself he felt no ability and willingness but rather heaviness and unwillingness, and he went toward the heavy cross of his impending martyrdom completely without comfort. Fearful that God had withdrawn his familiar favor from him, Glover complained to his friend Augustine and shared further with him that he prayed to God night and day but without experiencing any sentiment or feeling of God's comfort. Augustine answered: "You must await the Lord's will with patience, and, in spite of everything that you now experience, you must discern that your state is upright and good. You must continue firmly, as befits a man, not doubting that the Lord will visit you in his time, for I am fully persuaded that the Lord will fulfill your desire by enriching you with the full treasure of his comfort." Augustine left his friend with the request that as soon as he again became aware of the feeling of this comfort in his heart, he would indicate this with a sign, so that he could witness to it. All night he prayed for strength but to no avail. The next day the time came when he would undergo a martyr's death. Suddenly, while Glover found himself on the way and could already see the stake, he became so filled with God's holy comfort and filled with such heavenly joy that by clapping his hands he beckoned to Augustine and called, "Augustine, he has come, he has come!" This he did with such delight and liveliness that he looked more like someone who has been liberated from the danger of death to the freedom of life than like someone who must separate from this life through a painful death. Such was the change that the hand of God brought to this good man.

His brother, John Glover, was not a martyr, but he was a diligent believer of the gospel and also a godly man and more practiced in all spiritual trials. The same Foxe tells about him:

> It pleased God to lay his hand of inner anxiety and fierce suffering very heavily on him. Even though he was not destroyed externally by the fire like his brother and other martyrs, if we note what he felt and carried internally in his spirit and heart for such a long time, then he may be counted among the martyrs, along with his brother Robert. No less than his brother did he desire martyrdom. Actually, speaking comparatively, he could be considered a double martyr. No tongue can express what great anxiety and pain, what scorching heat from hell he felt internally in his spirit, when his brother Robert was quickly burned by the fiercest pain of the fire.
>
> I remember that I was with John once or twice, when he was young. I noticed, both from what I saw myself and from what he told me, that in five years he had so declined that there hardly remained any pleasure in him in food, sleep, enjoyment in life, or any other feeling. Indeed, I often wondered at the wonderful work that Christ performed in him. And if Christ had not now and then lightened the life of his poor, miserable servant, who was already so abandoned by him, by several gratifying comforts, it would have been impossible for him to endure the unbearable agony and pain.
>
> Actually, what gave rise to the condition in which he now found himself was not of such great weight. But this phenomenon we usually notice with the most saintly—the more godly they are, and the more they focus on the fear of God, the more they distrust themselves. It happens often that they are frightened by small matters, as if they were great mountains, while others are not in the least moved and frightened, even of the most terrible things. What gave rise to the condition was that he had begun to fall back somewhat into his former life, after he had been led by the light of the Holy Spirit to a knowledge of the gospel and had tasted a sweet experience of the heavenly kingdom of Christ.
>
> Because of this lapse he began to distrust himself, and he imagined that Hebrews 6 applied to him: "It is impossible for those who were once enlightened, and have tasted the heavenly gift, and have become partakers of the Holy Spirit, and have tasted the good word of God and the powers of the age to come, if they fall away, to renew them again to repentance, since they crucify again for themselves the Son of God and put him to an open shame" (Heb. 6:4–6). On the basis of these words he firmly imagined that he had sinned against the Holy Spirit, and he could not have doubted his salva-

tion more strongly than if he were in the deepest depth of hell. Every pious person can judge for himself what terrors, fears, and convulsions now filled his soul. However, it will always be difficult to form a correct judgment on this unless one has experienced it himself. When we now compare the agonies of the martyrs with John Glover's, then I ask: Which agonies, punishments, and flames would he not have wanted to undergo, if he only would have been able to enjoy some rejuvenation and refreshment? He suffered such unbearable pain of spirit that, even though he had no desire (and could not have) for any food, he still was forced to eat against his will so that he might postpone the time of his damnation as long as possible, because he thought that he would have to be pushed into hell as soon as his soul would leave the body. Even though he thought that Christ was filled with mercy toward him, he still imagined that Christ could not help him, because of the force of the word in Hebrew 6, where it says, *"It is impossible."*

I tell you all this not so much to expose his wounds and pains but that we all, having learned from his example, with him would praise the Son of God, who does not allow anyone to be tempted beyond his ability. To the contrary, Jesus tempers the evil that comes to us—so much so that he not only lightens what seems unbearable to us so that we can bear it but, above all, also turns the evil to our good, much better than we could think of ourselves. With no one is this so striking as with this pious servant of God. As we already noted, he had to endure such heavy trials and violent blows from Satan for many years. Nevertheless, at last the Lord (who had graciously kept him all this time) not only rescued him from all despondency but also brought him to such dying unto sin as one seldom sees. He was as one already placed in heaven and dead to the world, his heart having such abhorrence of sin that in word and thought he led a completely heavenly life.

Neither were his motives different from all the fruits of his whole life, since he never spoke a word that was idle or trivial. He gave the largest part of his lands to his brothers. He managed the rest through his servants so that he could spend his life quietly and devote himself to his divine studies, thus enjoying a continuous Sabbath rest.

Thomas Witte, a martyr in 1556, had been brought to denial and terrible recantation of the truth because of all kinds of threats. He himself testified what went on in his mind after this. He said:

During the night, following that day on which I had signed my recantation, I was deeply saddened, and I could not sleep because

> of the restlessness in my conscience. It is true that my body was now free from the chains in which I had been imprisoned, yet I found no joy or comfort. My conscience was distressed more and more every day, since I became convinced, by God's Spirit and Word, that listening to evil counsel had been the cause for my sin. This unrest of heart, added to the cruel mistreatment I had experienced, caused me to lie down ill.

When the guard urged Witte to allow Dr. Harpsfield to come to him, Harpsfield appeared with the document of the recanted doctrine in hand.

Witte said to him, "I am not satisfied, and I am especially assaulted in my conscience because of my signing. My conscience accuses me through and before God's righteous judgment and also through his Word; I feel that in my conscience, while Satan stands ready to devour me. I therefore beg of you, Master Harpsfield, return the signed paper to me, because I will not let my name stand." Witte goes on to write:

> He returned it to me and allowed me to remove my name; I was very happy about this, although I knew that the result would be my death. I was able to experience God's providence and grace for me in this event. It is true that God tests his people and allows them to fall, but he never allows that they be lost. In the midst of my temptation, God reminded me of what I had done, and he also rescued me. His name be therefore praised forever. Amen! Neither the devil nor the cruel tyrant can tear one of Christ's sheep from his hand.

Catherine Bretterg, a very pious woman (whose life and death is described separately and about whom Bolton tells several details), experienced the heavy hand of this spiritual abandonment on her deathbed. She often testified that it seemed as if there was a wilderness of many woes within her, that her sins made her a prey to the devil, so that she wished she had never been born and preferred to be any creature other than a woman.

She frequently cried out, "Woe, woe is me, poor, miserable, evil, abandoned woman," with the tears steadily flowing from her eyes. It is this same woman who was later delivered from her trials and came back to Christ and the enjoyment of his communion. Triumphantly she spoke these words to her beloved Savior: "O Lord Jesus, do you pray for me? O blessed, dear Savior, how wonderful, how wonderful are your gifts of grace! Oh, your love is indescribable, because you have dealt so graciously with me! O my Lord and my God!"

William Peacock, from England, was on his deathbed and contemplating all his earlier sins, which were not considered so great and many by others. He cried out, "Because of my sins I now feel a hell in my conscience. Oh, I am vile, my heart is wretched! Oh, how wretched and grieved I am! The burden of my sins weighs so heavily on me that I fear that my heart will break. Oh, how wretched and distressful is my condition that I must be harassed and surrounded by hellhounds." When the bystanders asked him whether he would not want to pray, he answered, "I am not able to." And to the question whether they should pray for him, he answered, "Please do not use the name of the Lord in vain by praying for a condemned person." But still, when the storm of trials was over, this same man testified, "Truly, my heart and my soul were taken far away and sorely pained by trials and stabs of conscience. I thank God that now they have much decreased so that I no longer desire to be branded as a condemned person." And later, when the trials were still fewer, he said, "Thanks to God, I feel so much comfort, and what shall I call it?" When one of the bystanders said, "Call it the good fight," he answered, "That is too small. Even if I possessed five hundred worlds, I would still not be able to pay for such a blissful outcome. The sea is not as full of water, the sun is not as full of light as the Lord is full of grace."

What happened to the Italian Pomponius Aligerius will be told later.

When Prince Maurice lay on his deathbed, Johannes Bogerman related two examples for his comfort. The first was about a minister who could not feel in his heart the trust in God's grace for which he so sorely longed. The other was about someone who complained that his heart appeared to be closed and turned to stone so that he could not discover in himself the remorse for his sins, such as he had felt earlier. However, with both it came to a good, comfort-filled, and blessed ending.

Andreas Fricius wrote about John Salesius, a Pole from Sendomir. On his sickbed, Salesius, driven by the dread of his conscience, frequently complained that he was not able to feel the power of Paul's word, "Those who are led by the Spirit of God are children of God."

Salesius thought that God's children should be driven by his Spirit, and those who are not so driven cannot be God's children. After this complaint about the absence of God's Spirit, says Fricius, Salesius heaved with such sighs that one could clearly notice how much he was abandoned by the Holy Spirit.

And so we could continue with relating examples. But whoever pays attention will see that such cases are not so unusual in the daily experience and temptation of souls. One will see this especially if he has been afflicted himself, for it is the same as with other illnesses—he will have the most interest in those situations that correspond to his. The telling and thinking about similar examples are very pleasing and beneficial.

From all that we have said about this we can now conclude the following: (1) that these trials are general and happen to every child of God, even the most holy; (2) why and for what good and blessed purposes God sends them; (3) how there finally always is a desired outcome of trust and deliverance granted to the soul. "If you endure chastening, God deals with you as with sons; for what son is there whom a father does not chasten? But if you are without chastening, of which all have become partakers, then you are illegitimate and not sons" (Heb. 12:7–8).

Fifth, to continue with the naming of comforts by which our souls can be helped and strengthened, we note that these trials sometimes do not last long. Your deliverance and joy is often much nearer and closer at hand than you think. The psalmist testifies to this: "For his anger endures but a moment, but a life in his favor; weeping may endure for a night, but joy comes in the morning" (Ps. 30:5). The Lord says to Isaiah, "'For a mere moment I have abandoned you, but with great mercies I will gather you. With a little wrath I hid my face from you for a moment, but with everlasting kindness I will have mercy on you,' says the Lord your Redeemer" (54:7–8). And in Isaiah 57, he says, "Thus says the High and Lofty One who inhabits eternity, whose name is holy: 'I dwell in the high and holy place, with him who has a contrite and humble spirit, to revive the spirit of the humble and to revive the heart of the contrite ones. For I will not contend forever, nor will I always be angry; for the spirit would fail before me, and the souls which I have made'" (vv. 15–16). The bride in the Song of Solomon cries out, "When I had gone past only a short distance, I found him, whom my soul loves" (3:4). For you also it may be "yet a little while, and he who comes shall come and not delay" (Heb. 10:37). Christ said the same in reference to his bodily return: "A little while and you will not see me, and again a little while and you will see me, because I am going to the Father" (John 16:16). "Brothers," said Athanasius, with an eye to the heavy persecutions, "it is a small cloud, and it will soon disappear."

Sixth, we note, finally, that these trials can be very useful and helpful. As we already demonstrated in chapter 1, they are very conducive to the way of salvation. Christ himself therefore testifies, "I tell you the truth, it is good for you that I go away" (John 16:7). And James writes in his letter, "Brothers, count it all joy when you fall into various trials, knowing that the testing of your faith produces patience" (1:2–3).

Usually one notices that a godly soul at one time, with reference to its salvation, is in a restful frame of mind but at other times is in a state of unrest when it is attacked and feels abandoned. The first state is more pleasant and lovely, but the latter is often better and more helpful and provides a more certain sign and proof of salvation. In the state of unrest, a person will watch over the soul more carefully, and while one otherwise might easily fall into carelessness, now he will be more diligent and more holy. After all, someone said about Christ himself, "Even though he was the Son, he still learned obedience from what he suffered" (Heb. 5:8). Robert Bolton says, "It is sometimes better to go down into the pit and there to weep about the loss of inner joy and comfort and to call out from the bottom of the deepest hell, 'My God, my God, why have you forsaken me?' than to go constantly hand in hand with the angels and to be, as it were, in Abraham's bosom and to have no other thoughts except about peace." And John Gerson testifies, "Often a dry soul is in a better situation than a restful soul." Thus, we note all those fruits that a person can again and again pluck from his distress. We must always, also in this regard, testify with King Hezekiah, "The word of the Lord that you [Isaiah] have spoken is good." He also said, "Should it not?" (2 Kings 20:19). Paul knew this and wrote to the people in Rome, "All things work together for good, for those who love God" (Rom. 8:28). Louis Paschal, a martyr in 1569, once said, "We do not so much need bread to sustain our temporal lives as the dear cross to strengthen our faith and to keep the hope of eternal life." Speaking about this cross, the Jewish Rabbi Gamse said, "This also is best."[2] And so it is. "For our light oppression, which passes very quickly, truly produces for us a very excellent, eternal weight of glory" (2 Cor. 4:17). Truly, "those who sow in tears will reap in joy. He who continually goes forth weeping, bearing seed for sowing, shall doubtless come again with rejoicing, bringing his sheaves with him" (Ps. 126:5–6).

2. The second source from which our comforts flow is God, as he reveals himself in relation to these trials and those who are tried.

Gregory says, "Comforts must be given not only in light of our situation but also with an eye to the righteousness of the Creator." In relation to God, the comforts can flow from his divine being, his divine attributes, or from God as he exists in the three divine persons.

Regarding the first, we read that David strengthened himself in the Lord his God. He comforted himself in God when the people of Ziklag wanted to stone him (1 Sam. 30:6). And God himself promised this comfort when he said, "I, even I, am he who comforts you. Who are you that you should be afraid?" (Isa. 51:12). And in Isaiah 66:13, "As a mother comforts, so will I comfort you." Polycarp called to his wife when she went to be tortured, "Remember the Lord."

Regarding the second, the divine attributes, you must remember that these trials do not come to you outside God's will but that they flow from his divine good pleasure, and that must be enough to put your heart at ease. Naomi complains, "Not so, my daughters, for it is more bitter for me than for you; the hand of the Lord has gone out against me!" (Ruth 1:13). Eli declares, "He is the Lord; he does what is good in his eyes" (1 Sam. 3:18). David says, "If I find favor in the eyes of the Lord, he will bring me back and show me both it and his dwelling place. But if he says, 'I have no delight in you,' here I am; let him do to me as seems good to him" (2 Sam. 15:25–26). Job cries out, "The Lord has given and the Lord has taken away" (Job 1:21). Christ prayed, "Father! If possible, let this cup pass by me, but not my will but yours be done" (Matt. 26:39). The church complains, "Why do you make us wander from your ways? Why do you harden our hearts so that we do not fear you?" And Augustine said, "We should rather be reprimanded if we do

2. Because of this expression he received the name Gamse, which means "this also is best" in Hebrew.

not will what God wills than that he should do or neglect something that is not good for us." Therefore, say with Polycarp, as he was tortured, "God's will be done."

Second, the trials flow from God's providence. On the basis of his divine good pleasure and wise rule (without which not a hair will fall from our heads), these trials come over your soul. Therefore, remember always that God does this, that he leads you into temptation, and say with Job, "Shall we receive good from God and not evil?" (2:10). Truly, there is no evil in the city that God does not do. With Jeremiah we say, "Let him sit alone and keep silent, because God has laid it on him" (Lam. 3:28). Tertullian once said, "By whom is the battle begun? By him who can imagine that he will also gain the crown and the prize."

Third, the trials flow from God's wisdom. God does not only send the trials but also rules and directs them with wisdom so that we can put our hearts at ease and can think, "Thus the Lord knows to deliver the godly from the temptation" (2 Peter 2:9). With the temptation he can also provide the escape so that we can bear it. Just as a teacher knows precisely which task he can assign to his student, and a physician how much he can give his patient so that the patient is then at ease and quietly entrusts himself to the hands of the physician, in the same way, yes, even much more so, we should consider ourselves safe in the exalted hands of our all-wise God and be comforted in these holy bitternesses that he sends to us. He shows his wonderful wisdom precisely in this, that, knowing how severe the suffering can become, he himself determines the degree of the fears and distress. In relation to Job, God first says to the devil, "See, all that he has is in your hand." After this, having strengthened his servant Job, God allows the devil more free rein by saying, "See, he is in your hand" but still adding this restriction, "but do not touch his life" (Job 2:6). God thus knew how he could continually increase the suffering of his servant. And just as he abundantly shows his incomprehensible wisdom in that he knows *what kind* of trials he must send to us, no less is his wisdom displayed when he knows how to direct these trials to a good end.

Fourth, the trials flow from God's goodness and mercy. Moses derived comfort from this when he said, "The LORD your God is a merciful God; he will not forsake you or destroy you" (Deut. 4:31). "Be strong and of good courage, do not fear or be afraid of them;

for the Lord your God, he is the one who goes with you. He will not leave you or forsake you" (Deut. 31:6). Jeremiah testifies, "Through the Lord's mercies we are not consumed, because his compassions fail not. They are new every morning. Great is your faithfulness. . . . Though he causes grief, yet he will show compassion according to the multitude of his mercies" (Lam. 3:22–23, 32). Also read Isaiah 63:9, where it says, "In all their affliction he was afflicted, and the angel of his presence saved them. In his love and in his pity he redeemed them, and he bore them and carried them all the days of old." But pay special attention to those comforting words and think about them with application to yourself, where God's mercy and loving-kindness toward your soul are described. For example, Isaiah says, "He will feed his flock like a shepherd. He will gather the lambs in his arms and carry them in his bosom and gently lead the mother sheep" (40:11). See also Isaiah 42:3: "A bruised reed he will not break, and smoking flax he will not quench." (See also Exod. 34:7; Ps. 103:8–9, 11, 13; Isa. 49:14–16; Hab. 3:2; Matt. 12:20; Luke 15:4–5.) Scripture therefore attributes (speaking humanly) "bowels of compassion" to God. Zechariah, John's father, speaks in Luke 1:78 of "inner movements of mercy of our God."

Fifth, the trials flow from God's faithfulness. God will not leave us, who are his, but, as he has always done, will also help us now. Paul writes, "No temptation has overtaken you except such as is common to mankind. But God is faithful; he will not allow you to be tempted beyond what you are able, but with the temptation will also make the way of escape, that you may be able to bear it" (1 Cor. 10:13). Hebrews 13:5 says, "He has said, 'I will never leave you or forsake you.'" God said to Jacob, "I will not leave you until I have done what I have spoken to you" (Gen. 28:15). That God's faithfulness is great is attested to on nearly every page of the Bible—just read 1 Samuel 17:37; Psalms 71:20; 86:13; Lamentations 3:22–23, 32; 2 Corinthians 1:10; 2 Timothy 3:11; 4:17–18. These are the comforts present in God's being and in his divine attributes.

Let us now, in the third place, see what comforts you can draw from the three divine persons, Father, Son, and Holy Spirit. In 2 Corinthians 1:3–4, Paul says about the Father, "Blessed be the God and Father of our Lord Jesus Christ, the Father of mercies and God of all comfort, who comforts us in all our tribulations." And in Romans 8:32: "He who did not spare his own Son but delivered him up for us all, how shall he not with him also freely give us all things?" And Jesus testified, "God so loved the world" (John 3:16).

The love and faithfulness of the Son comforts us. This love and faithfulness toward us is so great that Jesus is called "the comfort of Israel" and Paul must testify that "through Christ our comfort overflows" (1 Tim. 1:14), while Christ promises, "I will not leave you as orphans; I will return to you" (John 14:18). To that end, the Spirit of the Lord is on Christ: "To preach good tidings to the meek, to bind up the brokenhearted, to proclaim liberty to the captives, and the opening of the prison to them that are bound, . . . to comfort all who mourn, to comfort those who mourn in Zion, to give to them beauty for ashes, the oil of joy for mourning, the garment of praise for a distressed spirit" (Isa. 61:1–3). Paul could therefore write to the congregation in Thessalonica, "May our Lord Jesus Christ himself and our God and Father, who has loved us and given us everlasting comfort and good hope by grace, comfort your hearts and strengthen you" (2 Thess. 2:16–17).

The comfort of the Holy Spirit is of such a nature that comforting is ascribed especially to him, and for that reason he is specifically called "the Comforter." (See John 14, 15, and 16.) We read in Acts 9:31 that the congregation in all of Judea, Galilee, and Samaria walked in the fear of the Lord and the comfort of the Holy Spirit. Everything, whether it is from the Father, from the Son, or from the Holy Spirit, is contained in Paul's blessing: "The grace of the Lord Jesus Christ, and the love of God, and the communion of the Holy Spirit be with you all" (2 Cor. 13:14).

3. The third source from which our comforts flow is the holy gospel, in other words, that joyous message and that desired news for the weary soul from Christ and his saving grace. Paul writes to Titus, "But when the kindness and the love of God our Savior toward man appeared, he saved us" (Titus 3:4). Oh, how lovely is that name of Christ for a troubled soul! How full of comfort he is! The soul then repeats after the bride, "Your name is oil that is poured out. . . . We shall rejoice and be glad in you. We shall announce your excellent love. . . . A bundle of myrrh is my beloved to me, that lies all night between my breasts" (Song of Sol. 1:3–4, 13). O soul, look to your Beloved, to Christ, and see what he is for you, what he does for you, what he promises still to do for you.

When searching for who Christ is for you, you will find that he is God and man in one person. His divinity gives you everything, and his humanity leads you to confident communion with God. O soul, come to him; he is your brother, your eldest brother. Speak and claim freely, because his God is your God, his Father is your Father. He is flesh of your flesh and bone of your bone; it is he in whom all the fullness of the Godhead dwells physically, while you are perfect in him. He is also your mediator between God and by God, "for there is one God, and there also is one mediator between God and men, the man Christ Jesus" (1 Tim. 2:5). He is our high priest, who puts himself in the breach of God's anger and has satisfied for us with God everything that was necessary for our salvation. He takes away the certificate of debts that was against you; he breaks down the wall of partition that stood between you and God; he reconciles us with God in one body on the cross. "Through him we have access to the Father through one Spirit." He is our propitiation, our advocate, our intercessor. (See also Rom. 8:34; Heb. 7:25; 1 John 2:1.)

And finally, he is your Savior. Say with Paul, "This is a faithful saying and worthy of all acceptance, that Christ Jesus came into the world to save sinners, of whom I am chief" (1 Tim. 1:15). "Who is he who condemns? It is Christ who died and furthermore is also risen, who is even at the right hand of God, who also makes intercession for us" (Rom. 8:34). "Whoever believes in the Son has eternal life" (John 3:36). (Also read John 5:24; Rom. 8:1; 1 Cor. 15:55–57.)

When searching for what Christ does for you, you will see that he grants you grace. The first action of that grace is that he has called you to his knowledge and communion; without this knowledge you would never have had a true understanding of God or your salvation. "He who has saved us and called us with a holy calling" (2 Tim. 1:9). "God is faithful who has called you for communion with his Son, Jesus Christ, our Lord" (1 Cor. 1:9).

A second gift of grace is his justification. Through him, as if through your righteousness, you are acquitted of all your sins and the punishment you deserved in the terrible and righteous judgment of God. Truly, God does not will the death of sinners, and therefore, he has "set forth Christ for a propitiation through faith in his blood" (Rom. 3:25). When you consider this forgiveness, then you will notice that it comes from sheer grace and that the riches of grace are inexhaustible. Moses, therefore, when the Lord passed by him, cried out, "The LORD, the LORD God, merciful and gracious, longsuffering, and abounding in goodness and truth, keeping mercy for thousands, forgiving iniquity and transgression and sin" (Exod. 34:6–7). The poet of Psalm 103 testifies, "The LORD is merciful and gracious, slow to anger and abounding in mercy. He will not always strive with us, nor will he keep his anger forever. He has not dealt with us according to our sins or punished us according to our iniquities" (vv. 8–10). And in Micah 7:18–19, we read, "Who is a God like you, who pardons iniquity and passes by the transgression of the remnant of his heritage? He does not retain his anger forever, because he delights in mercy. He will turn again, he will have compassion upon us, he will subdue our iniquities. Yes, you will cast all their sins into the depths of the sea." You will also find that this grace is very spacious, and it covers countless sins because he forgives many times. You will further see that this grace includes full, complete forgiveness so that nothing remains. Micah says, "You will cast all their sins into the depths of the sea" (7:19), while the Lord promises, "I will forgive their unrighteousness and will remember their sins no more" (Heb. 8:12).

As a third gift of this grace we mention the adoption as children, and here we must distinguish between the adoption itself and the sealing of the adoption for the soul. Both are very comforting, and the apostle therefore thanks God the Lord fervently when he says, "Blessed be the God and Father of our Lord Jesus Christ, . . . having predestined us to adoption as children by Jesus Christ to himself, according to the good pleasure of his will" (Eph. 1:3, 5). John exclaims, "See how great is the love that the Father has given us, that we would be called children of God" (1 John 3:1). And Paul writes to the saints who are in Rome, "You received the Spirit of adoption by whom we cry out, 'Abba, Father.' The same Spirit bears witness with our spirit that we are children of God" (Rom. 8:15–16).

And if you consider what he has promised to still do for you, you will see that these promises on the one hand refer to a complete delivery from all evil, and especially from these trials. After all, he has promised never to forsake you. He has said, "I will not desert you, and I will not leave you." He has promised always to help you: "For he says: 'In an acceptable time I will hear you, and in the day of salvation I will help you'" (Isa. 49:8). Behold, now is the acceptable time, now is the day of salvation. He has promised to help you completely some day: "Oh, wretched man that I am! Who will deliver me from this body of death? I thank God, through Jesus Christ our Lord!" (Rom. 7:24–25; cf. Ps. 42:6; Isa. 43:1–2).

On the other hand, we also have the promise of complete salvation in the hereafter, because it is his good pleasure to grant you eternal life. John could therefore write, "Beloved, now we are children of God; and it has not yet been revealed what we shall be, but we know that when he is revealed, we shall be like him, for we shall see him as he is" (1 John 3:2).

Perhaps you now come with an objection and say, "But it is so burdensome, because it will be so long before the promise comes." If you sometimes cry out with the words of Luke 12:50, "How distressed I am until it is accomplished!" then I answer you also with a word from Luke: "By your patience possess your souls" (Luke 21:19). You will need patience, and he who is coming will come and not delay. "The Lord is not slack concerning his promise, as some count slackness, but is longsuffering toward us, not willing that any should perish but that all should come to repentance" (2 Peter 3:9).

Herewith we have discussed the three sources from which the abandoned soul can draw all comfort. The soul must remember and meditate on these comforts and consider them carefully. One must present the comforts forcefully to the soul that one wants to comfort. And not the least to be regarded as comfort is the fact that we have a Comforter. Just look at those who do not have this privilege. We read about the city of Jerusalem in the days of her misery in Lamentations 1:2: "She weeps bitterly in the night; her tears are on her cheeks"; she has no comforter. And David, in the person of Christ, complains in Psalm 69:20, "I looked for someone to take pity, but there was none, and for comforters, but I found none."

But against these comforts we have presented, the assailed soul has especially two objections that it usually brings up.

First objection. "Yes," says the soul, "those comforts are there and they are wonderful, but only for those who have a right to them. *They are not for me.* Since I do not belong among these fortunate ones, I have no right to them, and they are of no use to me."

Second objection. The soul uses this objection to reinforce the first one—that is, these comforts do not exert any power on the soul and produce no fruit. "I cannot," says the assailed soul, "apply any of these comforts to myself. Even though it is true that there are these comforts you described, they are not intended for me, because they do not help me."

What shall we say to this? To the first objection we answer: First, that the soul does not have sufficient grounds for what it says for and against itself, since it cannot prove it. Second, the soul's judgment counts less here; since it is involved in this struggle, it cannot offer a correct judgment about itself. It is like a sick person who during his sickness cannot follow his own ideas. Third, we have already proved with several powerful, godly, and sensitive arguments that this soul shares in God's grace (there are conclusive proofs present in the soul and these can be demonstrated), that it is a child of God, and that it has a right to all God's promises and comforts. Why now would the soul deny this against the truth and against itself? Fourth (and we will now offer no more proofs), I ask, would not the soul gladly enjoy God's comfort? In other words, does not the soul strive with all diligence and strength to be precisely that which it says it is not? The soul answers yes to this question. And that answer is precisely the proof of God's grace in the soul if it feels an unfeigned and heartfelt desire for the grace and goodness that it thinks and says is lacking. And that cannot be the case unless a person has true knowledge of himself and his failures, as well as of grace and its necessity. Such knowledge a person receives only through God's special grace.

But to ask further, Why does the soul say that it has no right to these comforts? The answer is, "First, because of my great and many sins, I am unworthy to receive these comforts; also, because I am rejected by God and abandoned, of which I have conclusive proof in my feeling." Concerning the first answer, that your sins are the reason you are not worthy of the comfort, my response is, first of all: What kind of an answer is that? Who is ever worthy because of his sins? Is not everyone who has ever been saved unworthy of salvation and deserving only punishment because of his sins? Is it not as the Lord says through Isaiah, "I am sought of them who did not ask for me; I am found of them who did not seek me. To a nation that was not called by my name I said, 'See, here I am, see here I am'" (Isa. 65:1).

Ask all of God's children, those still on earth or those already in heaven, and they shall unitedly confess with you that they are totally unworthy of God's grace. "But," you say, "my sins cannot be compared with theirs; the number of mine is much greater. There is no more horrible sinner, no creature more unworthy than I am."

When you speak thus, then I point you to Paul, who also confessed, "I am the chief of sinners," but added immediately, "however, I obtained mercy" (1 Tim. 1:15–16). So this is a common expression of converted sinners.

I note, in the second place, that it is a very good sign that you are very convinced of your sins and unworthiness. Bernard says, "A sinner must pray to God as a sick person to a physician. The prayer of a sinner can be hindered in two ways—either because he has no light or because he has too much light. The one who does not see or confess his sin has no light; on the contrary, he who is exposed to too much light regards his sins as so great that he begins to doubt forgiveness." Just so much light is good that you can know yourself, but it must not darken you or keep you from the true light. The centurion of Capernaum said aptly, "Lord, I am not worthy that you come under my roof." However, Augustine remarked correctly about this: "Calling himself unworthy made the centurion capable of Christ coming, not within his walls but into his heart. The centurion would not have said this with such faith and humility if he had not already carried in his heart the One whom he hesitated to let into his house."

Third, I point out how you not only see and know your unworthiness but now also lament it. Someone who spoke for Christ said to such a soul, "O daughter, it is enough for me that you suffer grief because you have sinned and that from now on you do not want to sin anymore. Now you are in a state of grace; what do you still fear? I am rich in goodness and mercy." Your heartfelt desire not to be such a great sinner and to be less unworthy is precisely the mark of all true converts. It is precisely from their lips that we hear the complaint, "Woe unto us that we have sinned," and they lament with Job, "Therefore, I despise myself and repent in dust and ashes" (42:6).

In the fourth place, I ask you, Do you dare to measure your sins and unworthiness against God's grace? Do you dare to stack them so high as if they cannot be forgiven and you cannot be helped? Remember the words of Paul in Romans 5:20: "Where sin increased, grace abounded much more." And Paul says elsewhere that he, the chief of sinners, obtained mercy so that Jesus Christ could show all his longsuffering in him, as an example to those who will believe in him for eternal life. And whereas Cain says, "My sin is greater than can be forgiven," Augustine remarks correctly, "Cain, you lie, because God's mercy is greater than the misery of all sins." Ambrose once said, "I judge that, because of such mercy of God, even Judas could not have been shut out from the forgiveness of sins if he had shown his remorse to Christ and not to the Jews." Chrysostom made the following remark:

> Your evil has a limit, but God's mercy and goodness do not. Your evil, no matter how great, is human evil; God's goodness, however, is boundless and will therefore easily win against your evil. If a spark of fire falls into the sea, it is doused and can no longer exist. As little as the spark is compared to the sea, so little, yes, even less, is human sin in comparison to God's grace and mercy, because the sea, no matter how great, has boundaries, but God's mercy and grace know no bounds.

And somewhere else he says, "Oh, how great are God's grace and mercy! Please do not say, 'I have sinned gravely; how could I be saved?' It is true—you cannot do it, but your God can, and he will do it so that your sins will be completely washed away." Basil also testifies, "If your sins are many, do not be frightened at the number, because where sins are many, grace is more abundant."

In 1555, the martyr Johannes Vernutius wrote from his prison, "Why would we not trust God from the depth of our hearts? Would our sins prevent us? Not at all. Because where there is much sin, there grace is more abundant, and the more sins are forgiven, the greater is the love of God. Or would our misery keep us from God? No, for the greater our misery, the greater also is God's mercy and help toward us. Then what would? Would our own illness hinder us? Not that either, since God's power is mighty in the weak, and the more we lack might, the stronger we are in him." The martyr Robert Glover, already referred to, also testifies, "O Lord, you confirm your might in our weakness, your wisdom in our folly, your mercy in our sins."

"But," says the soul in trial, "I have sinned here, and I have sinned there; my sins are so many and so horrible—oh, it is too much for me to mention them all!" My answer to that is: You have many more sins than you can mention. One more or less does not matter, because the number is immeasurably great. Take all your sins, also those you have committed unknowingly, or those that you thought would not count as sins, or those you have already forgotten—yes, take many more than you ever committed. What am I saying—"many more?"—you may as well add *all* the sins ever committed by people to your account. Then there certainly would be many more than you ever committed, and there still would be too few to stack up against God's grace. Compared to that grace the sins would disappear into nothingness. There always will remain the eternal dissimilarity between finite man and infinite God, to whom everything human, yes, everything outside of himself, is less than a dot. Never let your sins be so heavy to you that you would dare to place them in the scales to weigh them against God's grace and the power of the precious blood of his Son (Acts 20:28; 1 Peter 1:19). Truly, Romans 5:15 says it so clearly: "But the free gift is not like the offense. For if by the one man's offense many died, much more the grace of God and the gift by the grace of the one man, Jesus Christ, abounded to many." And in verse 17, Paul speaks on the one hand about the offense but on the other hand refers to the abundance of grace and the gift of righteousness through Jesus Christ. The ancients also speak similarly when they say, "Our sins are in descent and God's grace in ascent." It is therefore all wrong that you, because of your unworthiness, would separate yourself from Christ and his grace. On the contrary, you should, because of this unworthiness, go after Christ sooner and insist on this grace. Indeed, God wants to derive honor from his grace by showing that he renders it to the greatest of sinners; after all, prostitutes and tax collectors enter the kingdom of heaven before the Pharisees. And while Christ despises the Pharisees, he joins with tax collectors and sinners. "And the Pharisees, seeing this, said to his disciples, 'Why does your Master eat with tax collectors and sinners?' But Jesus, hearing this, said to them, 'Those who are healthy have no need of a physician, but those who are sick do. I have not come to call the righteous to repentance but sinners'" (Matt. 9:11–13).

Fifth, I observe that Christ came especially for such as these and renders his mercy to them! The more a soul realizes its unworthiness, its insignificance, and its failure, the more right it has to Christ and his grace. The invitation goes out to the thirsty and those who have no money. When the prodigal son had wasted everything, began to suffer want, and the complaint came from his lips, "I am dying of hunger," at that moment he stood up and went to his father and his father's house. Jesus grants his promise of grace to "all who are weary and burdened," to those "who are crushed in their hearts," and to those "who tremble before his Word."

Sixth, I point out to the soul that it may not offer any conditions to God and his grace, as if it would come earlier or would be more capable of coming if things were only different. Grace wants to be completely free and unfettered, and since it brings goodness, it does not look for that in man. The invitation to all thirsty ones therefore is, "Come to the waters, and you who have no money, come, buy, and eat. Yes, come, buy wine and milk without money and without price. Whoever is thirsty, come, and whoever wants to, freely take the water of life" (Isa. 55:1; cf. John 4:14; 7:37).

In the seventh place, I ask you, What ability do you think should first be present in you? And could you have that ability from yourself? Reasoning that way, you go in the wrong direction, and you incline to the harmful error that man can do something in his own strength, while he can really do all this only by God's grace (2 Cor. 3:5). And since this is true and always has been taught by the church of God, why should you then desire to have this ability of grace from yourself, since you can obtain it only by grace? Just read 1 Corinthians 12:3 and John 15:4.

Eighth, if you think that you please and oblige God more through your own ability, then you incline toward the detestable error of merit through works and the righteousness that results from that. And even though it is true that we have left popery, our human nature leans and rests too much on good works, as if those would give us more status, delight, and worth before God. Just like David, our soul must say to the Lord, "My goodness is nothing apart from you" (Ps. 16:2). We must look away from ourselves, especially from the imagined worthiness of our works, and "be found in Christ"; then we can also testify with Paul about "not having my own righteousness which is of the law" (Phil. 3:9).

Ninth, I must call out to the soul in all earnestness: When you find yourself in the state of trial and abandonment, then you are not free (as is sometimes thought) to come to Christ and take hold of his grace or not. Do not think that this is irrelevant and a completely indifferent matter whether you come or not. You should know that it is a sin, a grievous sin, if you do not come when God invites you (Matt. 11:28), loudly calls you (Isa. 55:1), commands you (1 John 3:23: "This is his command, that we believe in the name of his Son, Jesus Christ"), threatens you (John 3:36: "The wrath of God remains on him"), begs you (2 Cor. 5:20: "As though God were pleading through us, we implore you on Christ's behalf, be reconciled to God. For he made him who knew no sin to be sin for us, that we might become the righteousness of God in him").

So that you will not think that you are doing something differently from other people when you, with all your sins, find refuge in Christ and accept his comfort, I point you, in the tenth place, to all those who share in Christ and his comfort. You certainly believe that they also considered themselves unworthy of this benefit, do you not? Or do you think that they had more right to it than you? Definitely not! We already quoted what Paul wrote to Timothy (1 Tim. 1:15–16) and therefore point you only to what Peter exclaimed: "Lord, leave me, for I am a sinful person" (Luke 5:8). But this is what the Lord always does—he seeks and finds no others except sinners. When he went into Zaccheus's house, "all who saw it murmured and said, 'He has gone into the house of a sinful man'" (Luke 19:7). David therefore had to confess, "He does not deal with us according to our sins" (Ps. 103:10). Augustine made this confession: "Many and great are my ailments, they are many and great; but your medicine is much greater." And elsewhere he says, "I confess that I have sinned and that my conscience deserves damnation, and also that penitence is not sufficient for atonement; but your mercy conquers all transgression." Bernard speaks very comfortingly about this issue:

> Where is there more sure and more firm rest for those who are weak than in the wounds of the Savior? I therefore dwell safely with him, because he is mighty to save. The world rages, the body urges, the devil lies in wait, and still . . . I do not fall, because I am founded on a firm rock. I have sinned grievously, my conscience is distressed, but I will not be completely conquered, because I will remember the wounds of my Savior. He was wounded for my sins. And since nothing is so deadly but it can be helped by Christ's death, I cannot be

> frightened by the evil of any malady if I call up that strong and powerful medicine. So it becomes clear that he who once said, "My misdeed is greater than can be forgiven" was in error, unless he was not a member of Christ's body. Contrary to that, I freely accept everything that I lack from the wounds of the Lord, which overflow with mercy, since the openings from which all this flows are not lacking. They nailed his hands and feet, and they pierced his side with a spear, and through these openings I may suck honey from the rock and oil from the hardest stone, that is, I may see and taste how sweet the Lord is.

Although we have already dealt with this, we must discuss the following once more, because it is a complaint that the soul repeats so frequently. "Oh," the soul complains continually, "oh, my sins are so great and so many. I am the greatest sinner. And that is the reason that I have doubts and struggles and will perhaps perish. Oh, if I only did not have those sins!"

I will give a five-part answer to that. I ask you, first, where in the world could one find any person who did not sin, who did not sin frequently and grievously? Nowhere, of course. And how could anyone not sin? Who can bring forth clean out of unclean? There is only one without evil and separated from all sinners, namely, Christ Jesus; this cannot be said of anyone else. Holy Scripture therefore includes *everything* under sin and the curse when it says that the whole world is evil.

Second, I point to the very best among the saints. They also confess their sins and testify that they have committed the most sins and thus are the greatest of sinners. We know that about David, and we read that about Paul when he writes to Timothy that he, the greatest of sinners, has received grace.

I observe, third, that it is not good that we have sinned, and we must therefore ask with Job, "If I have sinned, what shall I do, O preserver of men?" It is good that we know what evil is in us, but we must also have a spiritual eye to see that evil. Everyone does not know his own evil and the extent of it; the ungodly lack that knowledge completely. We must see God's grace in the fact that we *feel* our sins, that we know them, but also in the fact that we *lament* them. Even though sinning in itself is a culpable deed on our part, the feeling, the knowing of our sins, is on the other hand the work of God's Spirit and grace. And now we must know not only our guilt but also the grace of God that works in us for our good. And this is precisely what we want to mention—that God's grace stands over against our sins for the easing of the soul in trial.

So we point out in the fourth place that a sinner, a feeling sinner, is truly the only object to which Christ shows all his friendliness, grace, and salvation. We hear from Jesus' lips, "Come to me all who are weary and burdened, and I will give you rest" (Matt. 11:28). Whom does he call? *All* who are weary and burdened. And what does he promise? To give rest to all of them.

Consider these words seriously and see what a great treasure of comforts and teachings for the soul they contain. In a different place in the Gospel of Matthew, Jesus says, "I have not come to call the righteous but sinners to repentance" (9:13). (See also Isa. 61:1–3; 1 Tim. 1:15; and other places.)

Fifth, put *all* your sins over against *all* God's mercies and *all* the merits of Christ, and then tell me if all your sins are not swallowed up and sink into nothingness in the abyss of God's grace, which he has revealed in Christ Jesus. Paul knew this too, and he could therefore testify in Romans 5:20, "Where sin increased, grace abounded much more."

However, the soul in trial has still more objections, on the basis of which it believes that it does not deserve the comforts, "because," it says, "in me is no virtue, no piety, nothing that is good. What can become of such a person?" To counter this objection I answer: Paul testifies the same thing when he says in Romans 7:18, "I know that in me, that is, in my flesh, nothing good dwells." Thus, we have this in common with Paul, and this complaint does not make our case more doubtful than his. Our wickedness is described in two ways in God's Word. Paul says in Romans 7:18 that *in* ourselves, in our flesh, no good dwells, and in 2 Corinthians 3:5 he says that of ourselves or *out of* ourselves we are not capable of anything truly good.

But then I ask, Did not God's grace and Spirit work a saving good in the soul in that complaint? Most certainly! First, that you realize and feel your failure so well—this is a virtue that you always have and is proof of God's grace and his illumination in you. Moreover, you have, besides this insight of your failures, also the humility that makes you see that you have nothing from yourself. In addition, you must not forget that a little virtue is still virtue. A small seed is still a seed—even a mustard seed grows into a large tree in which the birds of the air make nests. God, the Lord, working in us through Christ by grace, looks more at the genuineness of virtue than at its extent, more at the uprightness than its completeness—because the latter will be granted to us in the hereafter in Christ. Thus, Paul writes in 2 Corinthians, "A person is accepted according to what he has, not according to what he does not have" (8:12).

I observe, finally, that it is a generally occurring but praiseworthy desire in the pious always to strive more and more, to yearn for their spiritual progression, to long for perfection so that they do not value or ignore whatever they do have. Paul writes to the saints in Philippi, "But I press on, that I may lay hold of that for which Christ Jesus has also laid hold of me. Brothers, I do not count myself to have apprehended; but one thing I do, forgetting those things which are behind and reaching forward to those things which are ahead, I press toward the goal for the prize of the upward call of God in Christ Jesus" (Phil. 3:12–14). No one should therefore torture himself when he sees that he is not as holy as another or is not precisely as he would desire to be; after all, our desires cannot be satisfied, and that is just as well. The crumbs must satisfy us—God's grace, no matter how large or small, is always enough.

There is another objection when the soul says, "I have never experienced any conversion; I am always the same. However it is with other people, I am not converted." I answer to that: A person's conversion is known in four ways, which deal on the one hand with sin and on the other hand with righteousness—because the whole act of conversion is determined by the refraining from evil and the doing of good.

First, conversion is known in this, that the person lives separated and turned away, both from the evil life of other people and from his own sin. When he has an aversion to sin and avoids everything that is evil with strict scrupulousness, then he is certainly converted. The refraining from sin is certainly not yet complete in us, but it still is upright, and that uprightness becomes revealed in that all sins are avoided, although not always and not always with equal vigor. Also, not a single sin, even the one that conquers us most easily, our most personal and dearest sin, is excused. We say to each of those sins, "Go away!" As Ezekiel 18:31 commands us, "Cast away all your transgressions."

Second, conversion is known not only in the refraining from sin but also in the feeling of the inner slaying of the flesh, of the power and the desire to sin. Then a person not only refrains from sin but also does not want to do it; he even says that he cannot do it. Thus, John writes in his first letter, "He cannot sin" (that is, not through his own, full impulse), "for he is born of God" (3:9). It is that slaying, that crucifying of man, whereby the desire to sin, to speak with Isaiah, is destroyed "through the Spirit of burning." As Paul says in Romans 6:6, "That the body of sin might be destroyed, so that we will not serve sin." When something is slain in the soul, then the soul surely feels as if another person stood over against it—what Paul calls "the old man." And now the soul also considers how the desire to sin has been snuffed out and slain.

Third, just as this slaying is felt in relation to evil, so, on the other hand, the conversion is also seen in a making alive for good and for all virtue—the first brought about by the power of Christ's death, the second by his resurrection and his life. This making alive is a renewal of the inner man in understanding and will and inclinations so that he now possesses the knowledge to flee from evil and to follow the good. Now all his desire reaches out for God in Christ, and all his thoughts and desires are directed to fulfill all righteousness. Now he is what Paul calls a "new creation; the old has passed away, behold, all things have become new" (2 Cor. 5:17).

Fourth, conversion is known not only by making alive, or, as Paul calls it in Romans 7:6, "newness of spirit," but also by "walking in the newness of life" (Rom. 6:4). Thus, the conversion of man is shown most clearly when he, besides refraining from sin and practicing the good and the commandments of God, also shows himself very godly in his daily walk. Whoever diligently strives to refrain from all evil, who has died to sin and hates sin completely, who on the other hand feels a new life of the Spirit ignited in his heart and now tries to walk piously in everything—that person is certainly converted.

One can easily point to all this in the souls in trial and on that basis assure them of their conversion. It is, of course, something quite different to judge the truth, the extent, the growth of the conversion (I will now not discuss its perfection). Still, it is something quite different from passing judgment on someone's understanding generally or on someone who has been tried so violently that he cannot see or distinguish the most sure things that are really so obvious. Such a person is like Mary, who saw Christ and yet did not recognize him, or like Hagar, who was not aware of the well, even though it was right by her.

The soul makes yet another objection when it says, "There is no faith in me, and when faith is not present, there is no grace and no hope of salvation." My answer is: One need not here consider all the signs of faith and apply those to the questions of the soul, unless most of the signs, as well as faith itself, are denied by the soul. The most important thing one must do in this situation is to explain the *nature* of faith and explain it more fully and thus make clear to the soul what this nature of faith consists of. Imagine that there was a person who stated that he had no stomach, no heart, and no soul, while he lived, felt, and grew; would one then not have to explain to such a person the functioning of stomach, heart, and soul? It is the same with those people who do believe even though their faith is weak and attacked. Before anything else we must explain the nature of faith so they can feel they possess precisely that of which the power and functioning can be discerned and demonstrated. The soul needs, before anything, to know what faith, saving faith in Christ, is.

We briefly point out: (1) How the soul knows and understands that Christ Jesus, God's Son, is the *Savior,* the Jesus "who saves his people from their sins"; how he is the *only* Savior so that "no other name under heaven is given to men by whom they can be saved"; how he is a *complete* Savior, "who can save completely all those who go to God through him." (2) How the soul itself wants nothing more dearly and desires nothing more fervently than to be delivered and saved. (3) How the soul, from the strength of the first point, knows no other means for its salvation than the mediator, Christ Jesus. You do not put yourself up as Savior; you do not seek your salvation in temporary, worldly, and fleshly things; you know that you can and will be saved only through Jesus Christ.

From all this it follows that, if you doubt your salvation, you doubt either yourself, that is, whether you want to be saved, and that you cannot doubt because you know very well that you do want to be saved, or you doubt Christ, that is, whether he can and will save those who want to be saved and preserved by him. And you cannot doubt Christ, especially since you earlier already confessed that your faith in him was sincere. Thus, all of this shows that you have faith and that in deed and in truth you possess what you deny with your words: You have true and saving faith.

That you deny this faith flows from your ignorance about the nature of faith and from your lack of knowledge about the main points of religion. What is faith? What is understood by it? This—that Christ Jesus is the only one who can and will fully save us who want to be saved through him. "He who believes in the Son of God has the witness in himself; he who does not believe God has made him a liar, because he has not believed the testimony that God has given of his Son. And this is the testimony: that God has given us eternal life, and this life is in his Son. He who has the Son has life; he who does not have the Son of God does not have life" (1 John 5:10–12). In his Gospel, John writes, "These things are written so that you will believe that Jesus is the Christ, the Son of God, and so that believing you may have life in his name" (20:31). Through that faith within you there is a desire for salvation. This is the highest we aim for, and all those who in God's time will be heirs of salvation have this desiring, this heartfelt desiring. This desire comes only through a special grace and operation of God's Holy Spirit. Neither can this desire be present unless a person is also delivered from the bond and burden of sin and its curse, because only then can he lift up his head and long for salvation. This inner desire is proof of a good heart, of a heart that, tired of sin, is averse to the sinful state, a heart touched by God's Spirit and therefore looking for something better. "Blessed are those who hunger and thirst after righteousness, for they shall be filled" (Matt. 5:6).

This desire is accompanied by faith in the mediator Christ Jesus, through him and him alone, to reach this high and holy destination. This faith tells us that we understand and hold as truth what God testifies to in his Word, that is, that Christ Jesus, God's Son, alone can and will bring us to this desired salvation through his effective atonement and merits. This is faith, and it makes us say with Peter, "Lord, to whom shall we go? You have the words of eternal life" (John 6:68). Coupled with this, the heart gives itself completely to Christ, trusts that he is our Savior, that he will preserve us, that we are his, that we have been given to him and belong to him. These expressions demonstrate a trust that leans on and comes from faith. For this reason, you trust more than others that Christ is your Redeemer, your Savior, because you believe in him, while those others do not have that faith. You can exclaim with Paul, "For I know whom I have believed and am persuaded that he is able to keep my security, which I entrusted to him, until that day" (2 Tim. 1:12).

From faith flows next the assurance of salvation. Just as we trust that Christ will save us and that the trust relies on the fact that he can and will save all those who want to be saved by him, all those who go to God through him, in the same way we are assured that we will be saved in and through him. These things and deeds, in relation to the faith and whatever is connected to it, thus flow from one another. But the trust in the Savior and the assurance of salvation arising from the trust are the results of the real deed of faith. They are, as it were, the reaction, the echo, or the conclusion that follows from the principles. That trust and assurance are often hidden from the feeling of the believers as if they did not exist. They believe, but they still do not feel that they believe because the aftertaste of this trust and of this assurance is lacking. This, then, is the situation of the believers in trial.

However, we may not decide on the basis of this absence of feeling that faith is lacking, because faith can often be present, even though apparently all feeling of faith is lacking. It is the same as with the stomach, the heart, the life, which are not felt by many people, although they are present. Even though the trust and assurance are dimmed, still faith always remains in a person's being, just as during winter the life remains in the tree, although one cannot see either leaves or fruit. We prove our saying that faith always remains from the fact that the soul understands, holds true, and agrees with what Christ Jesus announces and promises in the gospel, that is, that he will and can completely save those whose desire is to be preserved and saved by him and him alone.

Besides what we have said about the essence and nature of faith, and that we have proved that this is present in the soul in trial, we can also point to the signs and circumstances of true faith, whereby our claim is further strengthened. Whether one looks at the *heart* that has faith and wherein faith is, as it were, laid away; whether one observes the deed and the *work* of faith; whether one beholds the power and the *fruits* of faith—one can take something from each of these to teach those in trial and persuade them that true faith is in them. As stated above, what you believe, you believe so sincerely that you would like to transform your whole heart into faith. This is not a faith of the lips or an empty faith but a faith of the heart. By this one knows and tests true faith, and precisely here we find whether faith is sincere. Thus, Philip also said to the Ethiopian, "If you believe with all your heart, you may be baptized" (Acts 8:37). Thus, you also want to believe with all your heart everything that is needed for your salvation. That is faith, that is true and upright faith, a faith that grants entry into the kingdom of heaven. If you observe the deed and the work of your faith, then you will see that your faith consists in this, that you reject, hate, and battle against all unbelief. Then choose. What do you want: belief or unbelief? Of course, you choose belief and not unbelief. You enter the lists against unbelief, you battle against it, and that would not be possible if there were no genuine faith within you. That you do battle against unbelief is not a sign of unbelief, because sin does not battle against itself. This is, however, a sign of belief, because sin is battled by its opposite virtue, which is of a completely different nature and thus in opposition to it. If you can pray, "Lord, help my unbelief," then you can also say, "I believe" (Mark 9:24).

If you look at the power and fruits of faith, then you will observe that these consist of love and good works. This love directs itself to God and spreads to our neighbor. Is there no love for God and neighbor in you? Examine yourself carefully. I know that God is the highest good that you desire and that you cry out nothing but "Oh, if I could only love him fully!" Remember the words of Jesus to the sinful woman, "Therefore, I say to you that her sins, which were many, have been forgiven, for she loved much" (Luke 7:47). From the proof of love one may therefore conclude that there is faith and forgiveness of sins through faith. Paul thanks God that he had heard about the Colossians' "faith in Christ Jesus" and their "love for all the saints" (Col. 1:4). Faith and love thus go together; they are, as it were, like twin sisters. You can therefore not say that you do not love the saints, because you esteem them highly, you seek their company, their virtue, their comfort, and their prayers. Where there is love in you for the saints, there you also have faith in Jesus Christ. The one does not go without the other.

The soul makes still another objection when it says, "There is no love in me for God." I answer: How can you say something like that? I will provide five proofs to make the opposite clear to you.

(1) Can you truly testify that the opposite of love for God is in you—that you hate God? That question frightens you! Why then do you say that you do not love God? Your inclinations are certainly not dead, not even without feeling. They are inclined either to God, and you love him, or they are turned against God, and you hate him. When you get to know something or someone, then the only outcome is that your will becomes inclined to that issue or that person either to express your affection or, if your mind judges differently, to flee that issue or that person. According to the knowledge that you have of God, you do not consider it good to hate God; to the contrary, you condemn that feeling as the worst evil. Thus, you do not hate God, but you love him.

(2) You do want God, that is to say, whatever you can desire in relation to God or from God you also want. Where there is such an affection in you, would love not also be there? You would wish that God be completely accepted, embraced, loved, served, and glorified by you. Your desire is that God accept you as his child, as his heir, and where you desire so heartily that you are God's and God is yours, would love not also be there? Do you not then say, "My beloved is mine and I am his" (Song of Sol. 6:3)?

(3) You also love him whom you fear, whom you are afraid to anger, because you do not so much fear your evil and the punishment you must undergo in God's anger as you do God's disgrace and displeasure. Thus, one fears only from love. Joseph said to Potiphar's wife, "There is no one greater in this house than I, nor has he kept back anything from me but you, because you are his wife. How then can I do this great wickedness and sin against God?" (Gen. 39:9).

(4) How can you say in your trials that you do not love God? All your laments are about the fact that God does not show you his love and favor; you long for that love of your God. And since you desire and love his love and favor, do you then not also love God?

(5) If you could buy that love of God, you would gladly give everything for it, whatever you possess. Since you would give everything for God and his love and be willing to lose everything, would

you be able to do that without love for God? Would one be able to say about such a person that he does not love God?

Still another objection says, "If there would appear to be any good in me, or even if it were really present, then that is nothing but hypocrisy, and therefore it will not please God to bestow those comforts on me." To that I answer: There is no more sure and obvious proof against hypocrisy than that a person himself laments about his hypocrisy. He who fears to be hypocritical is not so. To be afraid that this or that would be considered hypocrisy shows clearly an aversion and hatred for hypocrisy and also that one has no desire for or pleasure in such sin.

"But," you will say, "it could be hypocrisy, while I do not recognize it myself, since I deceive myself, which many people do in relation to themselves." To that I answer: Hypocrisy is that great mischief whereby a person either adorns his act with premeditated thought (and if he does this, then he knows it well enough), or he deceives himself with a righteousness that is not complete. If that is the case, then we can apply to that person what the angel wrote to the church of Sardis: "I did not find your works for God complete" (Rev. 3:2). Jesus says in Matthew 5:20, "For I say to you that unless your righteousness exceeds the righteousness of the scribes and Pharisees, you will by no means enter the kingdom of heaven." Precisely those persons show that they are not hypocrites who examine themselves carefully, evaluate themselves uprightly, think that their deeds are hypocritical, and are worried and fearful of that. He who is hypocritical makes sure that his deeds are seen and praised by people. But the person who really is not hypocritical is the one who strives to be pious (not for man or his praise but only with an eye to God) and who desires to live a godly life, even if there were not a person in the world who could see him.

Hypocrisy consists in three things. First, the heart is not inclined to those matters that are feigned. Jesus therefore says, "Hypocrites! Well did Isaiah prophesy about you, saying, 'These people draw near to me with their mouth and honor me with their lips, but their heart is far from me'" (Matt. 15:7–8).

Second, one does not, in hatred against all evil, strive to refrain from *all* sin but with premeditated thought makes exception for some sins and feeds them, while the commandment says, "Cast away *all* your transgressions with which you have transgressed."

Third, one is not diligent to walk in all virtues; one chooses to do certain things, while one refrains from others. This is opposed to uprightness. Not that a person can refrain from all evil *completely* and do all good *completely;* such striving he cannot achieve in this life. But one can be antagonistic to all sins, without excepting even one, and diligently given to all godliness. There always must be an upright desire to walk uprightly in all God's commandments—just as the whole sky is often illuminated, although not as completely as at noon, and just as a person is in all respects a person, even though he is not yet a fully grown adult. The Lord says, "Oh, that they had such a heart in them that they would fear me and always keep all my commandments" (Deut. 5:29). The uprightness of heart thus serves as a touchstone, and then it becomes clear that he who does not hold back any part of his heart, who has no desire to follow even one sin, who will gladly live according to all God's commandments, may not be counted among the hypocrites. He gives his *complete* heart to God; he tries to keep all his commandments; he prays that it may please God to work in him "both to will and to work, according to his good pleasure" (Phil. 2:13). The hypocrite cannot speak that way; he cannot do this heartily.

The soul sometimes raises a final objection during heavy trials to bring proof that it does not deserve those comforts because of its great and many sins. It says, "I am fallen away, fallen from God and God's grace." My answer is: God's Word teaches, to the contrary, that he does not permit his children to fall away totally. No matter what becomes of them, criticizing themselves and left to themselves, God, from his side, preserves them so that they will never be completely pulled from him, no matter how tried they are. Jesus himself testifies that no one shall snatch them from his hand. God's covenant, which he has made with believers, is an eternal covenant. He testifies through Jeremiah's voice: "And I will make an everlasting covenant with them, that I will not turn away from doing them good" (Jer. 32:40). God's eternal love flows from that covenant and is upheld by it. The Lord therefore says in Isaiah 43:4, "I have loved you," and he continues in verse 5, "Do not be afraid, for I am with you." The gifts of grace and the blessed gifts of God's Spirit in the soul therefore last until eternity; they are, to speak with Paul, "irrevocable" (Rom. 11:29). If someone laments that he has fallen away, it may be that he has fallen but impossible that he has fallen away. The fact that one knows his fall and laments it is certainly a sign that one is not completely cut off and that one does not live outside of grace, of feeling, of hope. John writes to the angel of the church in Ephesus, "Remember from where you have fallen" (Rev. 2:5).

In the second part of its "first argument," the soul says that it is rejected and deserted by God and therefore does not deserve his comfort. The soul asks with the words of Psalm 77, "Will the LORD cast off forever? Will he be favorable no more? Is his mercy clean gone forever? Does his promise fail for evermore? Has God forgotten to be gracious? Has he in anger shut up his tender mercies?" (vv. 7–9). I answer: Are you not saying something very wrong and ungrateful? Why are you lying against God? What does the Lord answer through Isaiah to Zion's complaint of "the LORD has deserted me, and the LORD has forgotten me"? The Lord says, "Can a woman forget her nursing child and not have compassion on the son of her womb? Surely they may forget, yet I will not forget you. See, I have inscribed you on the palms of my hands" (Isa. 49:14–16).

As we have shown you before, God proves his grace to you in many ways, also in the midst of these trials. How do you then dare to say, "God pushes me away"? God *cannot* do that; his goodness is a guarantee. Nehemiah testifies, "Nevertheless, in your great mercy you did not utterly consume them or forsake them, for you are God, gracious and merciful" (9:31). His steadfastness is also a guarantee of that. Certainly, God himself promises in Isaiah, "'For the mountains shall depart and the hills be removed, but my kindness shall not depart from you, nor shall my covenant of peace be removed,' says the Lord, who has mercy on you" (54:10). If the soul still says, "Yes, the Lord has rejected me," then I ask, how can that be, since he cannot wish this because of his goodness and he is not able to do this because of his steadfastness? Here you must keep in mind the warning of the theologians in their discussions of the "preservation of the saints": The foundation, the firmness of our spiritual state, must not be sought in man, as if he could keep himself so well and faithfully from falling away. Instead, we must find this in God, in Christ, who leads us by the hand and so supports and preserves us so that we will never fall away from his grace and from the state of grace. If all the powers of the world and of hell were united, they would not be able to do anything, not even against the slightest soul, if that soul is taken up into the covenant. Isaiah says, "You are my servant; I have chosen you and have not cast you away. Fear not, for I am with you; be not dismayed, for I am your God. I will strengthen you, yes, I will help you; I will uphold you with my righteous right hand" (41:9–10).

But the soul then says, "My *feeling* is only that I have been rejected by God." I answer: Neither you nor anyone else can know whether you are rejected by God; this can be known only from impenitence that lasts until the end and from sins that are unpardonable. However, this is not the case with you, because you have remorse over your sins and you fight against them. Why then do you speak so thoughtlessly? And I ask, from where does the feeling spring that you are rejected? Consider your argument carefully, and then you will note the opposite. If you were a "reject," you would not know what it means to share in grace, you would not feel the lack of it. You would not strive for grace or be concerned about its lack. Moreover, how many proofs have we not given you that you do possess grace? Would you now have a feeling only of evil and not of good or know only what you lack and not what has been granted? How unmannerly that would be! Would you yourself not find that ungrateful? You must therefore always have an open eye for what you possess, even if you feel nothing of this, and you must rejoice in that until the feeling also returns. You must then ask with Job, "Even if he killed me, would I not hope?" (13:15). Or say with the poet of Psalm 130, "O Lord, I call to you out of the depths" (v. 1). The soul knows that it still clings to God. And when the soul in trial might at times still ask with Gideon, "If the Lord is still with us, why has all this happened to us?" (Judg. 6:13), then we point to what we have said about this in chapter 1. Besides, when the soul searches itself, then it will find enough both in and outside itself to show that this trial is necessary and useful. A heathen already testified to this. Listen to Aulus Gellius, when he, citing Epictetus, says, "Not all those who must here undergo burdens are therefore hated by the gods; often there are hidden causes which are found by few."

Herewith we have refuted the first argument and the objections flowing from it. We now turn to the second argument that was brought up by the soul in trial.

"Agreed," the soul says, "that it is true that those comforts are not refused me, but what do they profit me, since I cannot apply them to myself? They do not exert any power on me or bear any fruit for me." Our answer is: This may be true, and the soul may find itself in such a time of drought, but it may not cast doubt on its whole state; instead, it must be patient. What God said to Israel through his prophet Amos also applies to this soul: "Because I will do this to you, prepare to meet your God, O Israel!" (4:12). The soul must bend itself under the strong hand of God and bear that until it can testify with Asaph that the right hand of God changes (Ps. 80:17).

But to be helpful to the soul in its search for comfort, we want to point it to some things for which it must watch out and some things it must do.

The soul must watch out for murmuring against God's hand and the trials he sends. It may not speak ill of God and the ways in which he leads but must say with David, "Surely I have calmed and quieted my soul, like a weaned child with his mother; like a weaned child is my soul within me" (Ps. 131:2). Isaiah cries out, "Woe to him who strives with his Maker! Let the potsherd strive with the potsherds of the earth! Shall the clay say to him who forms it, 'What are you making?'" (45:9; cf. Job 9:15; 42:3; Lam. 3:28–29). Gregory says, "He who murmurs about persecution accuses the righteousness of him who strikes. He who complains about the rod thinks that he is more pure than the Creator and considers inferior the One whose judgments about trials he criticizes."

Next, the soul must not refuse to be comforted, like Rachel, who wept about her children and did not want to be comforted; or like Jacob, who refused to be comforted over the loss of his son Joseph; or like Asaph, whose soul refused to be comforted; or like Jeremiah, who said, "My wound refuses to be healed." With Job the soul must say, "Teach me, and I will be silent. . . . Oh, how strong are right reasons" (6:24–25).

Third, the soul may not be suspicious or disbelieving about those things that can be obtained from God's Word for comfort so that it says with David in his haste, "All people are liars" (Ps. 116:11). From this it follows that the soul must not always look for objections and evasions of that which is faithfully explained—as if the soul always had to say something in opposition.

And finally, the soul must avoid always doubting and pulling down its state, which has been proven to be saved. Doing this is similar to what the apostle Paul says on another occasion: "Building up what I had destroyed" (Gal. 2:18).

This is what the soul must watch out for; and what must it now do? It must bind these comforts closely to its heart and open its heart for them, as for heavenly dew. The soul must, so to speak, suck up the dew so that the sap of the comforts flows from it. And since the burden is found especially in making the decision, in other words, in appropriating, one must especially dedicate oneself to that and help the soul. Jesus brought the disciple of Magdala to that point when he spoke to her with such emphasis and said, "Mary." That is how one must speak in the midst of the trial in one's soul: "Blessed are they who hunger and thirst for righteousness. I hunger for righteousness, and therefore, I am blessed." Since everything now depends on the conclusion drawn ("therefore, I am blessed"), and you must make that clear to the soul, you must frequently and strongly persuade the soul of the truth of the first part of the saying, "All who hunger for righteousness are blessed," as well as the second part, "I hunger for righteousness." The more you make this clear to the soul, the more the conclusion will become fixed in the soul: "Therefore, I am blessed." You must hold up this conclusion to the soul strongly and frequently so that it will not slide over that truth but *must* accept it.

As a means of bringing the soul to the appropriation of the comforts, we point to the soul's silently meditating within itself and the soul speaking to itself; these are of great importance. The saints of the Bible also used to hold these meditations. Thus, we read of David in Psalm 103:1, "Bless the Lord, O my soul, and all that is within me"; in Psalm 62:6, he says, "But you, O my soul, be silent before God"; we hear Mary say to Elizabeth, "My soul magnifies the Lord" (Luke 1:46). And when the poet of Psalm 42 experiences trials, he asks his soul, "Why are you cast down, O my soul, and disquieted in me? Hope in God, for I will yet praise him" (v. 5). In Psalm 16, it is David again who addresses his soul thus: "O my soul, you have said to the Lord, 'You are the Lord'" (v. 2). In Ecclesiastes 2:1, it is Solomon who testifies, "I said to my heart," and we read of Jeremiah that he said, "You, my soul, hear the sound of the trumpet" (4:19), and in Lamentations 3:24, the soul says, "The Lord is my portion." This is meditating *within* oneself, as David says in Psalm 143:5, "I meditate on the works of your hands." It is also recommended to speak to oneself, as we read somewhere in the ancients, "Listen, rational soul, companion of my reason, I want to say something *to* you that must remain a secret and concern between just us two."

The soul must also be busy with a serious and holy reflection on the holy sacraments that it receives. The reflection on both holy baptism as well as on the holy Lord's Supper will lead the soul to apply those promises of grace contained therein to itself. That is why the apostles continually remind Christians of the sacraments, as in Galatians 3:27; Ephesians 4:5; 1 Peter 3:21; and in Romans 6:3, where Paul says, "Or do you not know that as many as are baptized in Christ Jesus were baptized in his death?"

"But," says the soul, "I have enjoyed and experienced all of that unworthily, and therefore, it has lost its fruit for me." I answer: The fact that this unworthiness makes you sad and fearful is precisely a proof that the sacraments make their power felt in you, because they are intended to be of service to such as you. In addition, this is also a good sign, that your heart longs for the sacraments and that you strive to receive them more worthily.

And finally, one can properly point to the power of the keys, which are entrusted to God's servants. They must, according to God's command and in God's name, proclaim forgiveness of sins to such weary souls in trials. They may and must make use of the power of the keys to bring comfort to these comfort-longing souls—a comfort that is certain and sure and which they can apply to themselves (Matt. 16:19; John 20:22). They who are "servants of Christ and stewards of the mysteries of God" must, therefore, on the command of their Lord and Savior and according to their mandate, proclaim freedom and salvation, with strong reasons and firm foundations. That proclamation will undoubtedly exert a great influence on the soul and will serve to confirm the comforts that have been mentioned by us.

3

We discussed the comforts that can revive the soul in and under these trials; now we turn to the *means* that the soul must use against the trials whereby it can come to a blessed deliverance. "Is there no balm in Gilead? Is there no physician there?" The soul asks, "What are the means and where are they available?" Or it says with Thomas, "How can we know the way?"

We will silently bypass the physical means that can serve to purify one's constitution and strengthen one's being, since these are often injured or weakened through illness or other circumstances. Now we will speak to the spiritual person only about spiritual means, remembering Paul's words, "combining spiritual things with spiritual words" (1 Cor. 2:13). As we mentioned earlier about comforts, these spiritual means are either general (and can be used against all kinds of burdens) or special (to be used only by the struggling soul). We will discuss all these and consider:

1. those things against which the soul must be on guard
2. those things that precede the means and must be used
3. the good means themselves

1. Concerning the first—the things against which the soul must be on guard—these are either evil and wrong or they obstruct the good means. Since the soul is exposed to all kinds of temptations, there often arise terrible and evil things, which it seizes as a remedy. When the Lord had departed from Saul, he went to "a woman

in Endor who was a medium." It also happens that the soul in such a situation changes religion and joins another, a foreign religion. At times it occurs to the soul (as it did to Judas) to take one's own life in order to be permanently relieved from that situation. The Jesuits say that Ignatius, the founder of their order, refused to drink or eat anything until he had regained the peace that had gone from his soul; to that end he spent seven days in which he did not consume anything.

But all these things are wrong and must certainly be rejected and resisted. Such means produce a sense of revulsion. Thus, Elisha asked the messengers of the king of Samaria, "Is it because there is no God in Israel that you send for Baal-Zebub, the god of Ekron?" (2 Kings 1:3). And the Lord says through Isaiah, "I, I am the LORD, and there is no Savior besides me" (Isa. 43:11). Psalm 81 says, "Israel, if only you would listen to me! There shall be no foreign god among you, nor shall you worship any strange god" (vv. 8–9). The church testifies, "Our Savior's name is LORD of hosts, the Holy One of Israel!"

Baudartius tells about Doctor Nicholas of Greutzenach, a pious man, how on his deathbed he was violently assaulted because of his sins. After having sought help everywhere, he presented his good works to God—his going to mass diligently, his alms, the chastisement of his body, the cloister he had built for converted women sinners, and so on—but he found no comfort in any of these so that he often called out in great fear, "Will this not help me either?" Finally, with heavy sighs and weeping, he said, "Is there then nothing that can help me against sin, death, and the fear of hell? O God, my Lord, help me, have pity on me, for Jesus' sake, who was crucified for me." Soon thereafter he received comfort and abundant refreshment and peacefully passed away in the Lord.

The soul must, as much as possible, be on guard especially against three things. In the first place, against vain, heavy, difficult, wrong, and terrifying thoughts by which the soul is intensely tortured and assaulted. Job laments, "You disturb me with dreams and terrify me with visions" (Job 7:14). David said, "A fire burned in my musing" (Ps. 39:3); and Asaph, "I remembered God and was troubled; I pondered and my soul was overwhelmed" (Ps. 77:3). Make sure that your thoughts do not become master of your soul, govern it, take possession of it, torment it, and do with it what they want. But take care that you always bridle your heart and your thoughts, as Christ declares, "Possess your souls in your patience" (Luke 21:19). Just as one keeps horses under control though bridle and bit so that they cannot gallop or take us where they and not we want to go—in the same way, the soul must be bridled against impetuous urges and cravings of thoughts and inclinations by the reins of the spirit and all virtues. The prophet Jeremiah speaks of this when he says, "Wash your heart from wickedness, O Jerusalem, that you may be saved. How long will you let your vain thoughts lodge within you?" (4:14). And the wise poet of Proverbs wrote, "Guard your heart above all that is to be kept" (Prov. 4:23). The heart especially must be kept, because it, most of all, lies open to be attacked by all. It is just as with Abraham's offering that he could keep safe from the birds only with constant effort. Jerome says, "More than against anyone else one must be on guard against the devil," and Augustine confesses that the devil frequently brings filthy and evil thoughts into the soul just to bring it into confusion. A godly man once said, "Lord, my God, I am greatly tormented; I suffer grievously because many and harmful thoughts confuse me and pull my soul from you. Lord, it is an inner struggle and therefore so violent and dangerous since it is so close." Ephraim of Syria says, "Often filthy thoughts torment you; you are saddened by that, and you pray to God that he will deliver you from such a battle. Nevertheless, my brother, this torment is often very beneficial to you, and it frequently happens to you so that you will not elevate yourself but remain humble." In this situation, slanderous thoughts about God the Lord often arise in the soul—frightful thoughts about the faith and horrible thoughts about God. These thoughts also turn themselves against the soul itself in order to harm it, that is, to kill oneself. Read John Downame and Robert Bolton on this.

Here one must always make a careful distinction between what the devil infuses and what the heart brings against this. One must not immediately count it a sin against the person when such frightful thoughts arise in him. Paul says about this in Romans 7:20, "Now if I do what I will not to do, it is no longer I who do it but sin that dwells in me." Just as a virgin who is raped against her will, and as Jeremiah, who was taken into Egypt in spite of himself, so it is with the soul in spiritual trial; it is not the sin of him who suffers but of him who commits it. The soul that resists these thoughts is frightened by them and laments them. That soul is violated and does not have such thoughts from itself; they do not rise from within itself. These thoughts may not be counted as sin against this soul; on the contrary, they are a cross for it, a torment.

This distinction was firmly maintained by the theologians already mentioned and others. As Gregory also noted correctly, one must handle this issue very carefully. Thus, one must not dwell on such thoughts long or study them or discuss them at length or refute them. But as soon as one is aware of them, one must immediately put them away with, "Get away from me, Satan," and say no more than, "It is written." John Climacus said, "He who is upset by the spirit of slander and wants to be delivered from it can be sure that the cause of those thoughts do not lie in his soul but in the unclean spirit who once said to Christ, "I will give all this to you if you will fall down and worship me." We must therefore reject him and pay no attention to what he says but say boldly, "Get away from me, Satan." So as soon as these thoughts arise, they must be resisted. To speak with Jerome, you must not let these thoughts grow. Robert Bolton relates that someone who was in this situation answered the devil:

> You evil enemy of the honor of my God and of the peace of my soul, you disturb yourself and me to no avail. I confess about my Creator, Redeemer, and Savior—that he is an incomprehensible, glorious, wise, and gracious God; about heaven—that it is completely filled with holiness and blessedness; about creatures—that they all were created good by God's hand and are proof of God's great power, wisdom, and goodness; about Holy Scripture—that it is very holy and true and contains a rich treasure of heavenly wisdom and most sweet knowledge. But I also confess that you are the accursed one; you only are the author of all sins, of all damage, and of all difficulties that only you and yours deserve. Therefore, do not mix your wickedness with my humble, dear, and reverent thoughts about my Father, Savior, and Comforter.

One must further, as Cassarius notes, be busy with good thoughts in order thereby to be able to drive out the evil thoughts better and more firmly. Roman Catholics tell the following about Saint Catherine of Sienna. When she was tempted by the devil, especially when he said that she would not be able to persevere, she answered, "I do not lean on my own strength but on that of my Lord Jesus Christ." She said no more to him. She frequently admonished her friends that they, when tempted by the devil, should not argue with him, because, she said, "He is clever and through long practice so accomplished in deception that he already assumes the victory if he is permitted to speak to a person. Just as an honorable woman flees from an adulterer, so a chaste soul must turn away from the devil and turn to Christ, the Bridegroom."

In the second place, one must be on guard during the time of trial that one never neglects the exercise of one's calling wherein God has placed us. Satan is always trying to tempt us to neglect the exercise of our calling, because when we spend our time doing nothing, then we are more easily reached by him and our hearts will be most open to him. We must therefore always practice our calling with all diligence, just as we are accustomed to and just as is proper. Jerome gave this lesson: "Always do some work so that the devil will constantly find you busy." One cannot imagine what great advantage one gives to the devil if one spends his time in doing nothing. Just as it is necessary for one's physical life to keep busy with some work, so one must also be on guard that the soul is not found empty.

In the third place, one must be on guard not to neglect regular worship. Satan strives with all his might to push us so far that we have an aversion to the good and to the diligent practice of our worship—yes, to lead us so far that we say with Asaph, "Truly, I have purified my heart in vain." Worship may not be abandoned for anything. It must remain firm and must come before all other things, since it is always very necessary for everybody; one may never turn one's back on worship. No more than Boaz wanted Ruth to leave his field and therefore spoke to her, "Do not go to glean in another field; you shall not go from here, but you shall remain here" (Ruth 2:8), no more may the soul remain anywhere but in God's field in order to gather all comforts there. Job also testifies when he says, "My righteousness I hold fast and will not let it go; my heart shall not reproach me as long as I live" (27:6). David declares, "I have kept the ways of the Lord and have not wickedly departed from my God" (Ps. 18:21), while the poet in Psalm 44 says, "All this has come upon us, but we have not forgotten you, nor have we dealt falsely with your covenant" (v. 17).

Apart from the general necessity of worship, in the situation in which the soul now is, the person has a greater need for worship than ever in order to return to the earlier joy that God will again grant through a diligent practice of worship. God promises this when he says, "I will bring them to my holy mountain and make them joyful in my house of prayer" (Isa. 56:7). Thus, not *outside* but *inside* my house of prayer, not *without* but *within* worship. "If you refrain from trampling the Sabbath, from pursuing your pleasure on my holy day, and call the Sabbath a delight, the holy day of the Lord honorable, and honor him, not walking in your own ways, or finding your own pleasure, or speaking your own words, then you shall delight in the Lord" (Isa. 58:13–14). The soul must do as the bride did in the Song of Solomon—seeking her beloved everywhere and asking the watchmen, "Have you seen him whom my soul loves?" (3:3). And the worship that one practices in the midst of spiritual abandonment and dryness is rooted more deeply and is more disciplined than that which is experienced under the precious feeling of God's grace; it is proof that the person has come far in the denying of self and in the pure love of God and of worship—proof that what counts is God and not self.

One can read Franciscus Ludovicus Blosius about this. Among other things he says:

> The good that the person can do during these trials, even if it does not revive him, if he does what he can, is very pleasing to God. Let him therefore say to God, "Lord, if it were your good pleasure that I would be without any comfort until the day of judgment, then I would, by your grace and driven by pure love, be ready to bear all of that."

Blosius continues:

> Those people err who think that their works and their practicing worship pleases God only when they experientially taste communion with God and are made joyful by him. True perfection does not consist of the feeling of the intense and dear presence of God or the enjoyment of his comforts. Rather, we see it when a person leaves what is his, yes, leaves everything out of love for God, forsakes and mortifies himself, subjects his will completely to God's will, remains still and peaceful under everything that happens, and clings to God, having become one spirit with him.

Sometimes an objection is brought against this third means, being on guard against the neglect of worship: "Why should I still engage in worship practices? When I read the Bible, listen to the proclamation of the Word, or direct myself in prayer to God, then such strange and frightful thoughts come over me that it seems to me that I sin more in doing this than in neglecting it, that I make my evil worse instead of diminishing it." My answer to that is: Concerning those wrong thoughts, we have already spoken about them and pointed out that you may lament them as a burden that you must bear but that meanwhile you remain free from sin. And regarding the practice of worship exercises, you must not give in to the devil by letting him keep you from them. Because that is precisely his goal—to draw you away so forcefully that you listen to him and, if not completely at least partly, let go of your worship or slack off or become lax. No, always continue with, "only be strong and of good courage." Always keep the devil from you and continually use the weapon that Jesus wielded when he said, "It is written." If you do this, not once but always, and you persevere in that, then at last you will experience what happened to Jesus, as we read in Matthew 4:11: "The devil left him, and the angels came and served him."

2. In the previous section, we discussed those things that must, in this situation, be carefully avoided and renounced by the soul. Now we will look at those things that precede the good means and that must be used by the person. In that connection, we mention, first, a thorough examination of oneself and of one's sins. When doing so, the person will see that these come to him deservedly. The prophet Zephaniah urges this examination when he calls upon his people to seek the Lord, to seek righteousness and humility, and to remember the day of God's wrath (2:3). Jeremiah says, "Know what you have done" (2:23), and elsewhere, "What have I done?" (8:6). When there were three years of famine in David's time, he sought the face of the Lord to find out why this was happening. "And the Lord said, 'It is because of Saul and his bloody house, because he killed the Gibeonites'" (2 Sam. 21:1). In Jeremiah 31:18, Ephraim laments, "You have chastised me and I was chastised," while the next verse declares, "Certainly, after I was instructed, I struck myself on the breast." David therefore says, "I have considered my ways," and Job says, "Let me know why you contend with me" (Job 10:2).

Second, among these means must be reckoned a renewed, frank, pious, upright confession of one's sins. In Psalms 32 and 51, David gives the reason why he suffered such fear in his trial. He testifies in Psalm 32, "When I kept silent, my bones grew old through my groaning all the day long. For day and night your hand was heavy on me; my sap was turned into the drought of summer. I acknowledged my sin to you, and my iniquity I have not hidden. I said, 'I will confess my transgressions to the Lord,' and you forgave the iniquity of my sin" (vv. 3–5).

Baudartius tells of a rich man, hostile to the church, who, when he was sick and in a spiritual struggle, called the minister to him so that he might comfort him. The minister urged the sick man to confess his sins, but he could not persuade him. During another visit, while he still had not come to a confession of sins, the man asked the minister to read some comforting words from the Psalms. The minister agreed to this request and, as if directed by a miraculous divine guidance, opened the Book of Psalms to Psalm 32. After the minister had read this psalm, he expressed his astonishment and his joy that God had so guided him, and then he continued to draw several comforting thoughts from the passage for the struggling man. The man then cried out, "Oh, I feel that the hand of the Lord is heavy on me; I feel that my bones are perishing and my strength is shriveled and consumed, because I wanted to keep silent about my offense and conceal it from God and from people. Therefore, I now confess before God, before his holy angels, and before you, a servant of God, that I have sinned dreadfully. I agree, yes, I beg you, for God's sake, that not just you but all other ministers openly announce from the pulpit in the churches that I have confessed and lamented my sins. How good it is for me now compared to my earlier condition! I thank God that I have come this far. Now I have rest and peace in my conscience." The man died calmly some time after this. So it is: "If we confess our sins, he is faithful and righteous and forgives all our sins and cleanses us from all unrighteousness" (1 John 1:9).

A third means is a strong and firm intention from now on to live strictly and godly. David says in Psalm 51, "I will teach transgressors your ways" (v. 13), and in Psalm 22, "I will declare your name to my brothers; I will praise you in the midst of the congregation"

(v. 22). And Joshua announces, "As for me and my house, we will serve the Lord" (24:15).

Fourth, we must strive for thorough knowledge of and instruction in religion, for thorough knowledge of salvation and of the grace of God; there must especially be thorough knowledge of cases of conscience. We must also know the character and nature of spiritual operations and pay careful attention to our own and others' experiences and remarks. Through this knowledge, as Paul writes to the saints in Philippi, "your love may abound still more and more in knowledge and all discernment" (1:9).

It is told of Professor Franciscus Junius that he came to know a woman in the province of Limburg who had lived in utter despair for thirteen years and often cried out that she and her nine children were eternally doomed. She was brought to Junius after the priests had not been able to help her with their exorcisms and after the neighbors had found that the cause of her plight was that, because of her burdensome household, she frequently neglected to go to mass. Junius instructed her about the mass and explained to her that she had not sinned by not going to mass, and he further explained how she ought to live from now on. And to everyone's surprise, she was completely put at ease through this instruction, thus showing what thorough instruction in religion can achieve and how necessary it is. Upon examination we will always come to the discovery that many spiritual burdens come to a person through vast ignorance and inexperience about religion. Frequently a person understands so little about the basic articles of faith that he must first be instructed more extensively and better.

3. In the third place, we must speak about the good means themselves that can be used by us at the time of trial and spiritual abandonment. As such we mention:

First, contentment. One must learn to be content with those grace gifts and those spiritual, gracious blessings that God the Lord has already granted to our soul, in spite of our continual unworthiness. Also in relation to the spiritual life, we must learn to say with Paul, "I have learned to be content in whatever state I am. I know to be humbled and I know to have plenty. I have been instructed in everything, both to be satisfied and to suffer hunger, both to have plenty and to suffer need" (Phil. 4:11–13).

Second, patience. One must bear the hand of God with patience, testifying with Micah, "I will bear the LORD's anger, because I have sinned against him" (7:9), or with Jeremiah, "Let him sit alone in silence, for the LORD has laid it on him" (Lam. 3:28; see also Rom. 5:3; James 1:3; 1 Peter 1:6).

"But," you will say, "at times solitude is praised and recommended to a person; at other times it is forbidden. What is one to say to that, and what advice must one follow?" I answer this as follows: When one's emotions are strong enough, unassailed, and strengthened by God's grace and the power of his Spirit, then a person may well go into solitude. Yes, then it is even recommended so that his religious work may be completed unhindered and more fruitful. Tertullian says, "Our Lord Jesus himself often sought solitude in order to pray more freely and to be more separated from the world, and he showed his glory to his disciples in a lonely place." In Genesis 24:63, we read that Isaac had gone into the field to pray "toward evening." Toward evening, that is, at the time when it became deserted, he went to a deserted place to pray. Augustine says about this, "*Alone by himself,* in all stillness and when no one was present, except God and he." The Ethiopian reads from the prophecy of Isaiah and is instructed by Phillip after an angel of the Lord had carefully pointed out the place where he could find the Ethiopian, that is, "on the road that descends from Gaza, which is desert." Phillip thus found him in a very lonely place. "Oh," says Bernard, "that there were no person with me so that I might speak with God in the spirit (or inwardly)! He seeks separated and lonely places; therefore, I want to flee the conversation of people so that God can live in the innermost part of my heart." When a person is in that kind of situation, then solitude is recommended, yes, even praised. Jerome says, "Keep yourself in the most hidden places of your room and allow the Bridegroom to play inwardly with you there. You pray, you speak to the Bridegroom, he speaks to you." The same is said by Basil the Great, Ambrose, Chrysostom, and others.

However, for a struggling soul that does not stand firmly, that is not strengthened by God's grace and is open to the temptation of Satan, for such a one, solitude is not recommended, since Satan usually takes advantage of such an opportunity. Thus, he came to Christ in the solitude of the desert in order to tempt him. Thinking about the sadness and the burdens of the struggling soul, one can understand that it seeks solitude, because there it can more freely pour out its distress before God. Gregory says, "The more lonely, the more free." Jeremiah laments, "Oh, that I had a lodging place for travelers in the desert so that my soul might weep in the hidden places. Because of your hand I have sat alone" (9:1–2). And David heaves the sigh, "Oh, that someone would give me the wings of a dove! I would fly away to where I might stay! Look, I would roam far, I would stay overnight in the desert" (Ps. 55:6–7). But if we pay attention to the attacks of Satan, to the trials themselves, then it is not recommended to go into solitude, since we are afraid that the soul is too weak to resist the devil all alone.

One must therefore, as we said, possess one's soul in patience, "because you need patience so that, having done God's will, you may bear away the promise" (Heb. 10:36). If the soul has learned patience through these trials, then it has learned enough from it, as Paul also says that oppression works patience. "Yes," says Tertullian, "even if the whole world were destroyed—if I just gained patience from it."

Third, faith. One must lift up the heart through faith. Habakkuk says, "The righteous shall live by faith" (2:4), and Paul confirms this in Hebrews 10:38. He testifies of his faith in Galatians 2:20: "The life I live in the body, I live by faith in the Son of God, who loved me and gave himself for me." Luther comments on this passage, "Put all the emphasis and all the force on the words *'for me,'* and make it a habit to accept the words 'for me' in sure faith, to apply them to yourself, and do not doubt that you also belong to those who can say, 'for me.'" David says in Psalm 31:14, "But I trust in you, O Lord; I say, 'You are my God.'" This is the faith "with which you can put out all the fiery arrows of the evil one"; this is the faith "that conquers the world." The pious martyr, the widow of Waldrue Carlier, had the same faith when in 1555 they brought her the news that, according to the command of Emperor Charles, she would be buried alive, and she said, "Is that all you want to do to me? Very well! The Lord God himself pours out for each one the cup that he must drink, after God knows the strength of the person, and he will therefore also give me the patience." When Michiel van Doornick was led to the stake in 1547, he said, "I do not have to ponder long about this. He who did me the honor that I may suffer for his sake with patience will also give me the grace that I may with patience endure the pains of the fire." Dr. Luther said, when the devil showed him his sins, "These can also be forgiven, if I only have faith."

Fourth, hope. The soul must firmly hope in the Lord. The poet of Psalm 42 asks, "Why are you bowed down, O my soul? Why are you disquieted within me? Hope in God, for I will yet praise him. He is the help of my countenance and my God" (v. 5). Paul also points out that hope does not disappoint us. We see an example in the tribe of Judah, for "the children of the tribe of Judah were mighty while they leaned on the LORD, the God of their fathers" (2 Chron. 13:18). Job declares, "See, even if he killed me, would I not hope?" (13:15). And David says in Psalm 71:14, "I will always hope and will make all your praise still greater." (See also Pss. 27:14; 31:15; 40:2; 130:7–8.)

Fifth, waiting. The soul must wait for the Lord and his coming. Habakkuk said, "I stood at my watchpost and watched to see what he would say to me. . . . Though he tarry, wait for him, because he will surely come, he will not delay" (2:1, 3). Isaiah therefore says, "He who believes shall not haste" (52:12), and the blessed are therefore described as those who wait on the Lord, just as the great crowd of sick people in Bethesda waited for the disturbance of the waters (John 5:3). "Those who wait on the LORD will renew their strength. They will mount up on wings like eagles" (Isa. 40:31). Isaiah says, "Therefore, I will wait for the LORD, who hides his face from the house of Jacob, and I will expect him" (8:17). Micah calls it looking for the Lord: "Therefore, I will look for the LORD; I will wait for the God of my salvation. My God will hear me" (7:7).

The stargazing soul waits on the Lord and his gracious coming, as the paralytic in Acts 3, whose eyes were fastened on the apostles, "expecting that he would receive something from them" (v. 5), or as Christ commanded his apostles, "not to leave Jerusalem but to wait for the promise of the Father" (Acts 1:4).

Sixth, seeking. The soul must seek God and Christ. It must say with the church, "I looked for him whom my soul loves" (Song of Sol. 3:1). It traces him in all his ways; it tries everything if it may somewhere find and grasp him. And one never seeks him in vain if one seeks him with all his heart. The Lord himself testifies, "I have not said to Jacob's seed, 'Seek me in vain'" (Isa. 45:19), and he has said, "Seek and you will find" (Matt. 7:7; cf. Deut. 4:29; 2 Chron. 15:2).

Seventh, prayer. Most of all, the soul must call on him in prayer continually and thus seek him. It is therefore written, "That my people might humble themselves and pray and seek my face" (2 Chron. 7:14). The Lord says to Jeremiah, "So do not pray for this people or offer any plea or petition for them; do not plead with me" (Jer. 7:16). Praying to God is like calling on him, holding fast to him. The Lord said to Moses, "Let me alone so that my wrath may ignite against them" (Exod. 32:10). God considers himself bound through Moses' prayer so that he cannot carry out his punishment and anger. The only means and the only escape in that situation is prayer and steady sighing to God. David also does this in Psalm 38: "LORD, all my desire is for you, and my sighing is not hidden from you" (v. 9). We read about Manasseh, "When the LORD troubled him, he sought the favor of the LORD his God and humbled himself greatly before the God of his fathers. And when he prayed to him, the LORD was moved by his entreaty and listened to his plea" (2 Chron. 33:12–13). In Psalm 42, the poet says, "By day the LORD will command his loving kindness, and at night his song will be with me—the prayer to the God of my life" (v. 8). Asaph declares, "My voice goes to God and I call; my voice goes to God and he will incline his ear" (Ps. 77:1), and David declares, "I spread out my hands to you; my soul is before you as a thirsty land" (Ps. 143:6; cf. Ps.141:1–2).

Reading and meditating on the psalms of David in this condition are very beneficial acts and comforting for the soul, because they reflect very correctly its conditions. They tell us how the soul presents its needs and wants in the most powerful manner and how it calls on the Lord. Athanasius (or whoever may be the author of the work cited here) notes very correctly, "All God's Scripture certainly teaches virtue and true faith, but the Book of Psalms is like a mirror in which one observes the conditions of the soul."

Chrysostom says, "For that very reason the saints have always paid so much attention to the Psalms." Augustine tells about the power of the Psalms that he heard sung in the church of Milan—which especially facilitated his conversion. And John Hus says that he felt the real power of the Psalms for the first time in prison. John Morellius, a martyr in France (brother of the famous printer Wilhelmus Morellius), praises the prison in a writing in 1558, because in prison one can sing the Psalms so well and so unhindered. This agrees completely with the saying of one of the ancients, Hilary, that one hears more singing of Psalms in the dungeon than in the palaces of the great ones. Luther's wife declares that earlier she often did not know what this or that in the Psalms meant. She did not understand the laments, those operations of the soul, nor did she ever rightly understand her duty until God laid burdens on her and trained her through them. She said, "Oppression has been my teacher through which I learned."

Read the Psalms carefully, and there you will find the holy and correct manner of praying to God and calling on him in the midst of trials. Hear the poet of Psalm 102 pray, "A prayer of an afflicted man, when he is faint and pours out his lament before the LORD." When you explore the prayers of the saints of the Bible, you will note what reasons they use in their prayers, what a prayer should be like for this or that situation, how one really ought to pray, and why one must pray. With the prayers one intends either to ask for something good or for the prevention of something evil; in the situation in which the soul now finds itself, the prayers usually consist of both. We thus notice three things in prayer: (1) a presentation of and a complaint about evil, (2) a desire for the good and for deliverance from evil, and (3) the reasons to move God to deliverance.

The evil that the soul complains about is this: It seems as if it is forgotten or abandoned by God. Thus, the poet of Psalm 42 writes, "I will say to God, 'My Rock, why have you forgotten me?'" (v. 9). In Psalm 51, David prays, "Do not cast me from your presence and do not take your Holy Spirit from me" (v. 11), and Heman asks in Psalm 88, "Why, O LORD, do you reject me and hide your face from me?" (v. 14). In Psalm 22, the complaint is, "My God, my God, why have you forsaken me?" (v. 1; see also Pss. 10:1; 77:8–10.) The soul thus lays its burden before God in prayer, in its liveliest and strongest manner and so movingly that David testifies in Psalm 25, "The troubles of my heart have multiplied" (v. 17). We find the same in Psalm 55:3 and 33:10–11. Such prayer is accompanied by weeping and sighing: "I am weary with my groaning. All night I make my bed swim; I drench my couch with my tears.... My eye wastes away because of grief; it grows old.... Put my tears into your bottle; are they not in your book?" (Pss. 6:6; 38:10; 56:8; cf. 69:4; 126:5). In Job 16:20, we read, "My eye is dripping tears to God." The soul then also makes confession of its sin. David says, "I make my sin known to you, and I do not cover my unrighteousness" (Ps. 32:5), or as in Psalm 38, "I am miserable because of my sin" (v. 18).

The desire of the person praying, as in all other things, is that God will answer him and hear his prayer. David says in Psalm 55:1, "Give ear to my prayer, O God, and do not hide yourself from my supplication"; and in Psalm 27:7, "Lord, hear my voice when I call; be gracious and answer me"; in Psalm 28:1–2, "Lord, I call to you; . . . hear the voice of my supplication when I call"; Heman, in Psalm 88:2 says, "Let my prayer come before you; incline your ear to my crying"; and the poet of Psalm 85 says, "I will hear what the Lord speaks" (v. 8).

The praying person also asks for forgiveness of his sins. David asks, "Do not remember the sins of my youth or my transgressions" (Ps. 25:7). Job said about his trials, "You write bitter things against me and you make me inherit the unrighteousness of my youth" (13:26); therefore, he prayed for forgiveness: "Why do you not forgive my transgression and put away my unrighteousness?" (7:21; cf. Psalms 51; 130; 143).

Third, David prays to be delivered. "Deliver me from all my pursuers and save me" (Ps. 7:1; cf. 69:19). Finally, he prays that after this abandonment he may again experience spiritual joy and gladness. David prays, "Make glad the soul of your servant" (Ps. 109:28), and Moses asks in Psalm 90:15, "Make us glad according to the days in which you have afflicted us." Then again the prayer comes from the lips, "O Lord, make me alive for your name's sake." The soul desires all this in humility and despondency and on that basis dares to bear the despondent heart to God in order to obtain an answer. David pleads for this in Psalm 51:17: "A broken and a contrite heart, O God, you will not despise," and then trusts that God will hear his prayer. In Psalm 4:3, he says, "But know that the Lord has set apart for himself him who is godly; the Lord will hear when I call to him," and in Psalm 38:15, he says, "For in you, O Lord, I hope; you will hear, O Lord my God."

The reasons that the soul uses to move God to hear its prayer are varied. (1) The greatness of its misery. Then we hear the following: "Lord, lend your ear, listen to me, for I am miserable and poor" (Ps. 86:1). "My soul is weary of troubles" (Ps. 88:3; cf. Psalms 77; 86). Or with Jeremiah, "Lord, look at me, for I am in distress. My stomach churns; my heart is overturned within me" (Lam. 1:20).

(2) The soul points out, according to its insight and looking at the situation, that it is time. The question then comes from its lips, "How long?" (Pss. 6:3; 13:2), and the soul prays, "Bring your help in haste" (Pss. 22:19; 71:12). (3) The soul belongs to God. "Lord, do not be so very angry; do not remember the unrighteousness forever. Look and behold, we all are your people" (Isa. 64:9). Jeremiah therefore addresses the Lord as "Israel's expectation, its Redeemer in time of distress" (14:8). (4) God is gracious and merciful. The soul repeats after the poet, "Lord, remember your kindnesses and mercies, for they are from eternity" (Ps. 25:6). (5) The soul prays to God; the prayer is on its lips. "Hear the voice of my call. Lord, be gracious, for I call to you all day. O Lord, God of my salvation, I call to you by day and by night. I call upon you and my prayer comes to you in the morning" (cf. Pss. 5:3; 31:22; 86:6). (6) The soul trusts God and says with David, "Do not let me be ashamed, because I trust in you. . . . You are my expectation, Lord, my trust from my youth on—you who delivers those who trust in you" (Pss. 71:1, 5; 86:2; cf. Pss. 13:6; 17:7; 25:20; 27:7; 31:1, 14, 17; 77:2; 143:8). (7) The soul pleads God's promises. Solomon therefore says in his prayer, "Lord, God of Israel, there is no God like you, keeping covenant and goodness" (1 Kings 8:23). The poet of Psalm 71 pleads that the Lord give a command to save him (Pss. 77:8; 89:49). (8) The soul pleads that God has always helped in earlier times. "You have been my help" (Ps. 27:9; cf. Pss. 3:4–5; 22:4–5, 10; 77:6; 85:2). (9) The soul now also waits for God and his deliverance. "I wait on the Lord; my soul waits and I hope in his Word. My soul waits on the Lord more than those who watch for the morning" (Ps. 130:5–6).

In order to give more power to its prayer, the soul now adds to all of this promises whereby it binds itself closer to God and thus hopes to obtain from God more easily what it seeks so earnestly. The soul promises (1) to call on God always and to love him abundantly. "My praise shall be about you in a great assembly. I will pay my vows in the presence of those who fear him. . . . Keep us alive and we will call on your name" (Pss. 22:25; 80:18; cf. 43:4; 54:6; 56:12; 57:7). (2) To serve God more carefully in all the duties of obedience. David promises, " I will teach the transgressors your ways" (Ps. 51:13), and Jacob says, "The Lord shall be a God to me" (Gen. 28:21). (3) To dedicate some of what is his to God. So Jacob:

"And this stone that I have set up as a raised sign will be a house of God, and of everything that you will give me, of that I will certainly give you one tenth" (Gen. 28:22). We also read about Hannah: "She prayed to the Lord and wept copiously, and she made a promise" (1 Sam. 1:10–11).

This is the way that the soul must pray in its condition of abandonment. But it must not pray alone; it must also ask others to pray for it, according to the command of James, "Pray for each other" (5:16), and according to the duty of the Christian community. A certain Thalassius also obeyed this command when he wrote to his brother Paul, "Dear brother! Pray for me, because many disasters, that is, spiritual sadness and physical pain, are awaiting me—and I have deserved them." At the deathbed of Prince Maurice, Johannes Bogerman recounted the example of a godly man who complained during his illness that his heart was so closed, so stone-hard, that he could not, as he had earlier, have a feeling of abhorrence and sorrow for his sin and that he therefore many times asked a pious minister to come to him to pray for him. Then there came such a holy and blessed change that he thanked God humbly and heartily. Of such great power is the praying with and for one another.

Objection: "But," says the soul, "I have done all of that. I prayed many times, but I was not heard; my condition remained exactly the same; yes, perhaps it became worse. It is the same as with Job when he complained, 'I cry to you, but you do not answer me; I stand up, but you pay no attention to me' (30:20). I can say with Habakkuk, 'Lord, how long do I cry and you do not hear! How long do I cry to you, "Violence!" and you do not save?' (1:2)."

I answer you: Bernard said that there can be three reasons that prayers frequently remain unheard. These are either that they are not offered at the proper time, or that they are not presented as they should be, or that they do not happen where they should. Be that as it may, we do note that, even if the prayers were as they ought to be, God frequently lets the soul wait by not giving the desired result either immediately or in the way the soul desired. We have such an example in the Canaanite woman (Matt. 15:22–28). But when God postpones answering the prayer and thus tests the soul to see if it clings to him out of desire for the blessings rather than out of desire for himself, in the meantime, he gives something else with which he keeps the soul occupied and that is more blessed at that moment until it pleases God to grant deliverance and then gives it more abundantly, as the wait was longer.

In order to see rightly the truth of God's rich and full promise always to hear us, also when our prayer is refused, it is necessary that we think about and remember, first, that God, although he sometimes postpones for a long time, does not forget us, and second, that he maintains the freedom to change the desire according to his good will and for our benefit into something else or something similar, which is then usually better for us than that which the soul desired.

A person has the same freedom when someone else desires something from him. One often asks God for a stone, and then he gives an egg; one prays for a scorpion and receives bread. God thus gave Isaac instead of Ishmael to Abraham, and to David, instead of that illegitimate son for whom he had prayed so hard, a dear and blessed Solomon. Paul continually prayed during his trial when he was beaten with fists by Satan's angel. "I prayed the Lord three times that it might depart. And the Lord said to me, 'My grace is sufficient for you, for my strength is fulfilled in weakness'" (2 Cor. 12:8–9). Augustine comments on this passage, "See, the prayer that Satan's angel would be taken away was not heard. Why not? Because it was not good for Paul. Thus, he who was not heard with respect to the fulfillment of his desire was indeed heard with respect to his salvation." In another place, Augustine points to the prayer of the devils and says, "The devil is heard and an apostle is not heard? What do you think; how are the devils heard? They prayed to be allowed to go into the pigs, and it was permitted. And when the devil prayed to be allowed to tempt Job, his prayer was heard. Why then was Paul not heard?" The apostle himself answers this when he says, "And lest I should be exalted above measure by the abundance of the revelations, a sharp thorn in the flesh was given to me, a messenger of Satan to beat me with his fists, so that I would not be exalted above measure. Concerning this thing I pleaded with the Lord three times that it might depart from me. And he said to me, 'My grace is sufficient for you'" (2 Cor. 12:7–9).

So God hears the devil, whom he wanted to damn, and not the apostle, whom he wanted to heal, because the sick person sometimes desires much from the medications, which do not necessarily give what is desired. So it is with God. He does not hear according to what the person wants but whatever serves his health. God refuses because he judges that to be the best; he postpones so that the desire will become more fervent. Gregory says, "God refuses to help his children from their burden so that it will increase and that the desire will therefore grow, as is seen with the bride in the Song of Solomon 3 and 5." Therefore, persevere in prayer; pray without ceasing, and even if God postpones hearing, he will, however, not leave you, but in this desiring he will strengthen you. After all, "he gives courage to the weary and increases the strength of those who have no power" (Isa. 40:29). And in Isaiah 41, the Lord says, "I, the Lord, will hear them; I, the God of Israel, will not forsake them. I will open rivers in desolate heights and fountains in the midst of the valleys. I will make the wilderness a pool of water and the dry land springs of water. I will plant in the wilderness the cedar and the acacia tree, the myrtle and the oil tree. I will set in the desert the cypress tree, the pine and the box tree together" (vv. 17–19). That is, when your heart is still a desert, God the Lord will make a joyful pasture, plant trees, and will cause fountains of spiritual water to spring up. Therefore, do not slow down and do not fall down; things will change, and "he who is to come shall come and not delay."

However, remember that it is not yours to know "the times or seasons that the Father has put in his own authority" (Acts 1:7). But do as the disciples did and expect the promise of the Father. Do not despise prayer, even if God does not hear at once, "because," says Bernard, "God does not despise it either, but before it has left your mouth, he has already written it in his book." We can undoubtedly expect one of two things: Either God will give us what we have prayed for or he will give something else that is of more benefit to us. Therefore, think the best of God and the worst of yourself. Yes, even more, you must believe about him more than you can imagine. The martyr John Hooper prayed an excellent and powerful prayer in 1555: "Lord, I am hell, and you are heaven; I am a filthy pool of sins, but you are a gracious God and a merciful Redeemer. Therefore, be merciful to me, a miserable and evil offender, according to your great mercy and invaluable goodness. You have ascended to heaven; take up my hell and make me share in your joy, for you sit in the same glory with your Father."

Eighth, stirring up to take hold of Christ. The soul must encourage itself to incline to Christ and to do everything to take hold of him and his grace. Isaiah speaks of this when he says, "There is no one who calls on your name, who stirs himself up to take hold of you, for you have hidden your face from us" (64:7). And David says, "My soul, hope in God" (Ps. 42:5, 11).

Ninth, companionship with the pious. It is very beneficial that in that condition of abandonment one seeks companionship and fellowship with several faithful and devout friends, especially with a minister, preferably someone who has much knowledge of and is experienced in similar cases of conscience. He should be one who is able to comfort and who is, as it says of Apollos, mighty in the Scriptures. The Lord asks by the mouth of the prophet Nahum, "Where can I find comforters for you?" (3:7). Jesus himself, when he felt abandoned by everyone, sought the companionship of his disciples and asked if they could not watch with him one hour. And when people left him, "an angel from heaven was seen by him and strengthened him" (Luke 22:43). Solomon, in the Song of Solomon, describes how the church, having lost Christ and vainly looking for him, turns to the watchmen and asks them for advice: "Have you seen the one whom my soul loves?" (3:3). And the word that Paul writes in his second letter to the Corinthians applies to all: "Who comforts us in all our tribulation, that we may be able to comfort those who are in any tribulation with the comfort with which we ourselves are comforted by God" (1:4). In his *Book of Martyrs*, John Foxe relates that when Rowland Taylor rode to the place of judgment, a poor man with his five children came walking toward him, and, while they all kneeled and stretched out their hands, the man said, "O dear father and good shepherd, Dr. Taylor, God help you now as you many times helped me and my poor children."

But when the situation is of such a nature, as sometimes happens, that there are no comforters or ministers, then God himself fills that place and grants his inner and immediate comforts, more abundant to the degree that external comforts are lacking.

The History of the Bohemian Persecutions offers a beautiful example of such comfort. When Hendrik Otto van Loss, one of the Bohemian directors, had received the verdict of death, he said to the minister Rosacius, who was visiting him:

> Oh, how glad I am, man of God, that you have come to me. Now I can let you share my joy and tell you what happened to me. I was just sitting in my chair and was very troubled that none of my ministers was present to offer me absolution and to serve the Lord's Supper, and I was sad that I had not had the benefit of your service. Falling asleep with these thoughts, my Savior came to me and said, "Let my grace be sufficient for you, for I cleanse you through my blood." He let a small drop of his blood fall into my heart, from which I awoke and jumped up. You can freely believe that I felt a wonderful reviving in my heart. Then, raising my hands high, I spoke, "I thank you, gracious Savior, that you have given me such comfort and thus wanted to assure me of your grace. Now I understand what is meant by 'Believe and you have eaten.' Now I no longer fear death, but I die with joy."

Let us now hear and answer several objections that the struggling soul makes against that which we have said about and to it. When the soul is in that situation, there are disputes that take place continually, and these can be so violent that one can hardly believe it.

First objection: "Everything that you have said and advised I have already done, and yet I am not helped. What is now my power that I should hope?"

Answer: If ever in any burden a person comes back constantly to the same thing and always complains about the same thing, that is certainly true in the situation of abandonment. But one can understand this, for one persistently puts one's hand where he feels the pain, and the mouth speaks continually out of the overflow from the heart. And I must say with Paul, "For me to write the same things to you is not tedious, but for you it is safe" (Phil. 3:1).

Therefore, in addition to what I have already said, I point you to the *promise* in Isaiah 30: "Therefore, the LORD will wait so that he may be gracious to you. And therefore, he will be exalted that he may have mercy on you, for the LORD is a God of justice. Blessed are all those who wait for him. For the people shall dwell in Zion at Jerusalem. You shall weep no more. He certainly will be gracious to you at the sound of your cry. As soon as he hears it, he will answer you" (vv. 18–19). Also remember what David commanded his son Solomon in 1 Chronicles 28:9: "And you, my son Solomon, know the God of your fathers and serve him with a devoted heart and with a willing soul, for the LORD searches all hearts and understands all the intent of the thoughts. If you seek him, he will be found by you; but if you forsake him, he will cast you off forever." David cries out to you in Psalm 103:9, "He will not always strive with us, nor will he keep his anger forever." Isaiah says, "For the LORD will comfort Zion, he will comfort all her waste places; he will make her wilderness like Eden and her desert like the garden of the LORD. Joy and gladness will be found in it, thanksgiving and the voice of melody" (Isa. 51:3; cf. 54:1; 55:13; 60:15).

In the second place, I point you to the example of others. Paying attention to their trials, you will see that no matter how long the struggle lasted, the outcome was always blessed. We say with Moses, "Ask about the former days that were before you, from the day that God created man on the earth" (Deut. 4:32). Asaph also did this. He says in Psalm 77:5, 11, "I have considered the days of old, the years of ancient times. . . . I will remember the deeds of the LORD; yes, I will remember your wonders of old." The poet of Psalm 44 also witnesses, "O God, we have heard it with our ears, our fathers have told us" (v. 1). And David speaks completely in the same spirit when he says in Psalm 22:4–5, "Our fathers trusted in you; they trusted and you delivered them. They cried to you and were delivered; they trusted in you and were not ashamed."

In the third place, pay attention to your own experience. Bernard says, "The soul pants hard and prays without ceasing and torments itself with desire to see if God, whom it desires so much and whom it seeks so diligently, will be so merciful that he will come. That soul may, I think, from its own experience repeat after Jeremiah, 'You, LORD, are sweet to those who hope on you, the soul who seeks you,'" and the prophet Habakkuk asks, "Are you not from of old the LORD my God, my Holy One? (1:12)." The story is told of the martyr Wolfgang Schuch of Lotharingen, when he, in 1525, climbing the stake, was asked if they should ease his pain somewhat replied, "The good and merciful God has been with me throughout my life, and he will certainly not leave me in this last hour when I have the greatest need of his help." When they lit the fire around John Berraud in 1556, he called out, "My Lord and my God, now reach out your hand to your servant."

Second objection: "I am finished. I am beyond hope and cannot be helped; I despair greatly and lament with Jeremiah, 'My strength is gone and my hope in the LORD.'"

Answer: When you speak about despair, you must make a distinction between despairing and to be assaulted and tried with despair. It is not at all the same if I say, "I am severely assaulted to despair," or "I am despairing," because the devil often attempts to drive the most pious to despair; this is testified to by Robert Bellarmines and John Downame, but they did not despair.

You must also distinguish between despair about oneself, about being able to help oneself, and despair about God, as if he were not mighty enough to lend help. The four lepers found themselves in the first kind of despair when the one said to the other, "If we say, 'We will enter the city,' the famine is in the city, and we will die there. And if we stay here, we will die also. Now then, come, let us surrender to the army of the Syrians. If they keep us alive, we will live; and if they kill us, we will only die" (2 Kings 7:4). Such is a blessed despair that is also found in conversion, as with the prodigal son (Luke 15:16–17) and with the multitude on the day of Pentecost (Acts 2:37).

One must also pay attention to the distinction between being perplexed and being in despair. Paul makes that distinction when he writes in his second letter to the Corinthians, "perplexed but not in despair" (4:8). You must further make the distinction between despair in words and despair in deeds. It may be that because of his heavy attacks someone speaks the words of a despairing person, even though he does not really despair. Gregory says, "Often the words of the righteous are the same as those of the unrighteous, but the meaning of both is very different." Finally, there is a great difference between to despair for a time and almost to despair and to do so continually and fully.

Now that we have established these distinctions, we ask, second, why and for which reasons would you despair—you who have reason only to trust and hope? Will one such burden, and a burden that is so minor, be able to separate you from your God? Should you not rather conquer, yes, more than conquer? Would you not prefer, with Abraham, to "believe against all hope" rather than "throwing away your confidence, which has a great reward of life" (Heb. 10:35)? Thomas à Kempis says, "When comfort has been taken from you, you must not immediately despair, but wait for the heavenly visit with humility and patience, because God is powerful to grant you more grace and to give you grace again." Augustine says, "Who, dear Jesus, would despair of your grace? I really dare to say that no other transgression is such a serious sin as to despair of you."

Third, I point out to you that God does not will that you despair. That is why the prophet Ezekiel had to say to the house of Israel in the name of the Lord, "Thus you say, 'If our transgressions and our sins lie upon us, and we pine away in them, how can we then live?' Say to them: 'As I live,' says the LORD GOD, 'I have no pleasure in the death of the wicked, but that the wicked turn from his way and live'" (18:22–23). In his commentary on Psalm 51, Augustine has David say, "Have pity on me, O LORD, according to your mercy. What I have done is wrong, but I flee to you, the Almighty. I would doubt at the sight of my deadly wound if I did not have you as my Physician." His daily prayer was, "Lord, bestow on me that grace that I may learn to know you and myself rightly—that I may learn to know myself as the poorest sinner and you, on the other hand, as the loving God, who is my gracious Father for Christ's sake."

I note, fourth, that you cannot say that you already despair and doubt. If you lament with the church of Jeremiah's time, "My strength is gone and my hope in the LORD" (Lam. 3:18), then you must also say with her, "This I recall to my heart; therefore shall I hope" (v. 21). You certainly do not believe that your salvation is impossible. You do not feed doubt by agreeing with it, do you? Instead, you oppose it forcefully and fight against it, do you not? You esteem Christ and his grace highly, lifted far above all earthly things, do you not? You do not reject that grace or cut it off, do you? Instead, you look forward to it with great longing. Well, if this is so, then you do not despair. God will not permit you to be devoured by too great a sadness. However desperate your situation may appear to you, it does not appear so to God—not to God, who (to speak with Isaiah) "shall prepare a road in the desert and rivers in the wilderness" (43:19). Paul Millet, a martyr in the year 1564, says, "When a Christian feels that God's hand rests heavily on him, then he must not doubt but must rather be joyful and remember that all this comes from the hand of a good Father, who does not want his child to be lost."

Third objection: "Well, be that as it may, I am still afraid that I may fall into that situation; as David says, 'One of these days I will be killed by Saul' (1 Sam. 27:1)."

Answer: Our answer can be short. We have already pointed out that, because of the firmly abiding and persevering divine grace, as well as the preserving and indwelling of the Holy Spirit, this is impossible; it has never happened, and it will not happen to you. After all, "'the mountains shall depart and the hills totter, but my kindness will not depart from you, nor will my covenant of peace totter,' says the Lord, who has mercy on you" (Isa. 54:10). Isaiah 50:10 says, "Who walks in darkness and has no light? Let him trust in the name of the Lord and rely upon his God."

Fourth objection: "I am afraid that it will become so bad that I will go insane."

Answer: Since we do not know ahead of time what will happen to us, it is foolish to torture oneself already with an evil that is still not sure. It is certainly not likely that the result will be insanity. The senses and the mind are not so readily injured completely; on the contrary, it often happens that the senses become more alert and more steeled through sadness. And even if this disaster would strike you, this still would not hinder your salvation. One judges simple or insane people according to their earlier condition and according to the deeds they performed before this simpleness or insanity. And if someone is simple or insane from birth, then one bases his judgment, out of love, on God's covenant, which includes believers and their seed. However, whatever happens to you, do what David advises and "commit your way to the Lord and trust him; he will do it" (Ps. 37:5). Do what Peter says and "cast all your cares on him, for he cares for you" (1 Peter 5:7). St. Dorotheus (a sixth-century monk) relates in his letters that a certain man understood very well the words of Matthew 6, "Do not be worried about tomorrow."

Fifth objection: "But what if I were to die in the condition in which I now find myself? What if David's prayer ('Spare me, that I may recover strength before I go hence and am no more' [Ps. 39:13]) remained unanswered?"

Answer: If you were to die while still in that condition, your salvation would not be less certain or less sure; no, it would probably be more sure. Salvation does not depend on the feeling that one has about it but on the truth of saving grace in us, even if that is not felt. Some people fall peacefully asleep in the Lord, while others are, as it were, taken up in a fiery chariot. But what difference does it make *how* one gets to heaven—the question is *whether* one gets there. Roman Catholics relate that when Johann Tauler was near death, he gave up the ghost under the most severe trials, even though he had lived piously. His friends were very concerned about his condition after death, since he died in despair. This fear (note carefully that this is added by the Roman Catholics) was discarded when Tauler appeared to one of them and told him that the devil had tormented him fiercely in the final hours of his life in order to drive him to despair. However, this did not happen; by God's grace he overcame the devil's trials, and, taken up by angels, he was brought into the heavenly realm, where he now enjoyed eternal bliss because the angels had forgotten to take him to purgatory. Be that as it may, it is still certain that good and pious people (insofar as others can judge this) can die in a state of spiritual insensitivity. But usually one sees that God offers abundant refreshment and comfort to these souls before their death. That is why Job prays, "Stop! Leave me alone so that I may have a little comfort" (7:16).

It is told about Everard, Duke of Wittenberg, that three days before his death he had such heavy trials that he could hardly speak. When after this he was delivered from this battle, he thanked God and said, "Lord Jesus Christ, Son of God, I know that it is your will that people believe in you. Because you said in your Word, 'Come to me all who are weary and heavy laden, and I will give you rest,' I call on you, and I commend myself to you, and I ask and await eternal salvation from you. Forgive my sins that clung to me during my reign, as well as my other transgressions."

We will silently pass by those other people about whom we already spoke. But we do want to point to John Holland, about whom Bolton relates that the day before his death he was busy for two hours with a meditation and explanation of Romans 8. Suddenly he called out, "Stop reading! What is the light I see? Do you have candles over there?" And when the person who was reading to him said that it was sunlight (it was summer and five o'clock in the afternoon), Holland called out, "No, it is not the light of the sun but of my Savior. So, farewell world! Welcome heaven! The morning star from above is visiting my heart! Oh, tell this after I have left and proclaim it in my funeral sermon. God is so intimate with man. I feel his grace. I see his glory. I do not know whether I am in the body or out of the body—God knows—but I see inexpressible things." The following morning at daybreak, he rose, leaned on his staff, as Jacob once did, and breathed his last, after he spoke the following blessed words:

> Oh, what a blissful transition will I have! It is a passing from night to day, from darkness to light, from death to life, from sadness to comfort, from a vain world to a heavenly existence! Oh, my dear brothers, sisters, and friends, I am sorry to leave you behind, but remember my death after I have left. And I hope that what I feel now will also be experienced by you before you die, that is, that God deals very intimately with people. And now, fiery chariot that came down to get Elisha, also carry me and bring me to that blissful place. And you, blessed angels, who are waiting for the soul of Lazarus to take it to heaven, carry, oh, carry me into the bosom of my Beloved. Amen. Amen. Come, Lord Jesus, yes, come quickly.

The Lord sometimes allows the soul to descend into hell but then also carries it out of there again—and that during this life. As terrifying as the first is, the latter is greatly desired, yes, much more wonderful. Then man triumphs over hell from which he is delivered and over heaven in which he is placed. Everyone can imagine how lovely, how comforting it is, especially just before death, to see heaven opened and already to taste the heavenly joy in one's heart. That indeed is heaven on earth! Then the desire arises in one's heart, "May my soul die the death of the righteous and my end be like his" (Num. 23:10). Then one says with Augustine, "You already do so much for us in prison—what will you do for us in the palace?" Then one exclaims with David, "Oh, how great is the good that you have laid up for those who fear you!" (Ps. 31:19). The following is told about Bernard. When he seemed to be near death, it seemed to him in ecstasy of spirit that he stood before the judgment of God. Satan was also there and brought ungodly accusations against him. After the devil had said everything he could, Bernard, addressing the devil without hesitation, answered, "I confess that I am not worthy and that I cannot obtain the kingdom of heaven through my own merits, but my Lord Christ possesses that kingdom through a double right—through the inheritance from his Father and through the merit of his suffering. He is satisfied with the first and he presents me with the other. Thus, I credit the kingdom on myself as his gift and am not ashamed." Thus, he conquered his enemy, and the man of God came to himself again.

Wessel Gansfort, also called Basilius, died in 1489. When one of his friends came to visit him when he was on his deathbed and asked how it was with him, Wessel answered that considering his illness and his age (he was then over ninety years of age) it went fairly well but that one thing caused him great distress, that is, through various thoughts and arguments he had begun to doubt the Christian faith. His friend was shocked at hearing these words; he earnestly admonished Wessel and then left. But what happened? Several hours later Wessel came to himself again and then said to the friend who had returned, "I thank God; all those vain disputes have been swept away, and I know only Jesus and him crucified."

Olympia Fulvia Morate, a learned and widely famous woman who died at age twenty-nine, was asked before her death if she felt troubled by anything. Her answer was, "At least seven years ago the devil tried with all his might to pull me from the faith. But now it seems that he has lost all his power and does not show himself in anything. And in my heart I feel nothing but the full rest and the full peace of Christ." As she lay in bed with her face beaming with joy, her husband asked her why she was so joyful. She answered, "During my rest I saw a place filled with beautiful and excellent light." When she was not able to speak further, her husband said, "Be of good courage; you will live in that beautiful light." She then nodded in agreement and said laughingly, "I am very joyful," and soon thereafter, "I do not know you anymore; now everything seems to be filled with beautiful flowers." She died in the year 1555.

We have already spoken about Luther's trials. He commonly testified about himself, "We are all doing well, except Luther himself; being healthy in body, he is tried externally by the whole world and internally by the devil and all his angels." He was also wont to say that "three things make someone into a theologian, that is, reflection, prayer, and trials." According to Justus Jonas, who was then with him, at one time Luther was so severely tried, simultaneously in his body and in his soul, that he, thinking only that he would die, made his will and testament, which sounded as follows: "Lord God, I thank you that you have willed that I would be poor on this earth. I have no field, possessions, or money that I leave. You have given me wife and children, whom I return to you. Feed them, teach them, keep them, as you have done for me until now, O Father of orphans and Judge of widows."

The next day Luther said to Justus Jonas, "I will always remember yesterday. Yesterday I was in the training school, and I sat in a hot bath of sweat." Later, he frequently spoke of this trial to his friends and called it *Colaphum Satanae,* that is, a "fist punch from the devil," as Paul speaks in 2 Corinthians 12:7 about the angel of Satan, who would beat him with fists. Justus Jonas, Luther's faithful fellow servant and fellow minister who was with Luther at his death, also experienced such a severe trial before his death that he was nearly beyond comfort. However, by means of many and extended comforts and admonitions from his servant, he was strengthened and was again victorious.

Luther's final conversation with his friends dealt with the question as to whether we will know one another in heaven. This made such an impression on his student Johannes Matthesius that he wrote his last sermon about this same topic, in reference to "the raising of the young man from Nain."

Luther died soon after this. When one of the bystanders read something comforting from Luther's own writing, Luther said, "Do not read my explanations now. If I had felt then as I do now, I would have written differently. Everything you say and read does not affect me." However, after this he was set straight and was comforted; in this comfort he died peacefully and devoutly.

When Martin Bucer lay on his deathbed, and John Bradford, on his way to the pulpit, said that he would pray for him, Bucer said, crying, "Lord! Do not reject me in my old age when my powers are leaving me. Chastise me forcefully, but do not reject me." When he was admonished to arm himself against the devil, he said, "I have nothing to do with the devil; I am only in Christ. Far be it from me that I would not now feel that sweetest of all comforts."

Casper Olevianus, professor and minister in Heidelberg, told on his deathbed of a certain vision and a certain thought he had received. He said, "Yesterday, after the departure of the two young dukes, I was, as it were, drenched with great delight for four hours and more so that I wondered why my wife and mother still asked if I was feeling somewhat better. Really, it could never be any better. It seemed to me that I was walking in a beautiful field where I was overwhelmed with heavenly dew—not in drops but in great abundance and out of full bowls from which I derived great joy in body and soul." Piscator then said, "The Good Shepherd Christ Jesus brought you into his pasture." "Yes," Olevianus then said, "he brought me to the fountains of living water."

When Salomo Gesner, professor in Wittenberg, was on his deathbed, they read to him about comforts against the devil's trials. Gesner said, "I have absolutely nothing to do with the devil, and he does not make it difficult for me during my illness. Just let him come; let him attack and test his powers against me, a poor sinner—but I will not become fainthearted by all that because I know that I have not sinned against him but against God. Thus, following the example of the Israelites in the wilderness, I will point the devil to the brass serpent, although that will not help him. I will point to the Son of God, hanging on the cross, and I will say to the devil, 'I have sinned against that One and not against you, and I entrust myself to him completely. I believe that just as he paid for the sin of the whole world, he also paid complete atonement to the Father for my sins. So get away from me, devil! Aim your arrows at Jesus, this seed of the woman. If you can conquer him, then you have also conquered me.'"

The following is told about John Knox, the Reformer of Scotland and minister in Edinburgh. They asked him how it was with him and why he sighed so deeply. He answered:

> I have undergone many battles and trials from the devil in my frail life, but now this roaring lion comes at me most violently and pours all his powers on me at the same time to devour and corrupt me. First, he frequently displayed my sins to me, then he often tempted me to despair, and he also tried repeatedly to ensnare me in the temptations of the world. However, being dashed to pieces by the sword of the Spirit, that is, God's Word, he was not able to accomplish anything. He now attacks me in another way, and that evil serpent tries to tell me that through my faithfulness in service I have earned even heaven and blessed immortality. But praise be to God, who has given me Scripture passages such as, "What do you have that you have not received?" and "I am what I am by the grace of God," and "Not I but the grace of God in me." I killed him through these words and extinguished that fiery arrow so that he left defeated. Thus, I thank God through Jesus Christ, who has willed to give me the victory. Now I believe that the devil will no more assail me but

that I, after a short time, without great distress of body and fear of spirit, will exchange this mortal and miserable life for eternal and blessed life through Jesus Christ.

Thus, one sees through all this how God, the Lord, is wont to give his children refreshment and comfort through the certain experience of their salvation, even after the most severe trials before their death. As Robertus Rollocus said before he died, "How fearful it is to fall into the hands of God, but mercy has been laid up for me in Christ Jesus. Why are you cast down my soul? Why are you disquieted in me? Soon you will share in the most dear face and the most beloved conversation." King Henry VIII of England said when he lamented his sins on his deathbed, "But the grace of Christ is strong enough to forgive all my sins, even if they were much greater than they are."

4

After this the Lord answered Job out of a storm" (Job 38:1). Thus, God finally comes back to us whom he had abandoned and answers us. Augustine says, "You who are good and almighty, you care for each one of us as if you cared for only one, and you care for each one as you do for all." God was not in the wind or in the earthquake or in the fire, but he came in the rustling of gentle quietness (1 Kings 19:11–13). We have spoken of the nature of spiritual trials, of the comfort and of the help to come out of those. Now we want to speak of the deliverance itself and end with that.

"Comfort, comfort my people, says your God. Speak to the heart of Jerusalem and call to her that her warfare is accomplished, that her iniquity is pardoned" (Isa. 40:1–2). Thus far Christ kept himself, as it were, behind the wall and looked through the bars; now he breaks through as a sun through the misty clouds and haze that hung over our dark and dejected soul; now he shines on and revives the soul. "Who will show us any good? O Lord, lift the light of your countenance over us" (Ps. 4:6). Psalm 18:28 says, "For you will light my lamp; the Lord, my God, will lighten my darkness." Here the soul is illuminated and also warmed by a godly ray of light from above, yes, from God himself, who proves his favor to that longing soul. "Arise, shine, for your light has come, and the beauty of the Lord rises over you" (Isa. 60:1). Just as the rain comes on the thirsty and dry earth, so here God pours "water on the thirsty and streams on the dry ground" (Isa. 44:3; see also Job 29:23). And it is "as the cold of the snow in the time of harvest, . . . as cold water on a weary spirit" (Prov. 25:13, 25), or, as it says in Isaiah, "as a clear heat that dries the rain, as a cloud of dew in the heat of the harvest" (18:4). That hour must be that long expected hour, for thus says the Lord, "In an acceptable time I will hear you, and in the day of salvation I will help you" (Isa. 49:8).

Gregory says, "Three times there will be a turning in the spirit of every elect person when he regains joy and comfort after bitter sadness and fear, namely, in conversion, in trial, and in death. And as great as the pain is on the one hand, so great on the other hand will be the joy." What an unspeakable and unending pain it was to the soul to be so abandoned by God and from the experience of his favor. The soul was abandoned in such terrifying trials, since the devil aimed at the lone, poor soul, fought against it, and trampled and nearly tore it apart in his evil and tyrannical will. David prays in Psalm 22:20, "Save my soul from the sword, my lonely soul from the violence of the dog."

However, Isaiah says, "I greatly rejoice in the LORD; my soul will be joyful in my God, for he has clothed me with the garments of salvation; he has covered me with the robe of righteousness, as a bridegroom decks himself with priestly ornaments, and as a bride adorns herself with her jewels" (Isa. 61:10). Jesus says, "A woman, when she is in labor, has sorrow because her hour has come; but as soon as she has given birth to the child, she no longer remembers the anguish because of her joy that a human being has been born into the world. Therefore, you now have sorrow, but I will see you again, and your heart will rejoice, and no one will take your joy from you" (John 16:21–22).

"Sing to the LORD! Praise the LORD! For he has delivered the life of the poor from the hand of evildoers" (Jer. 20:13). And as David says, "Blessed be the LORD, because he has heard the voice of my supplications! The LORD is my strength and my shield; my heart trusted in him, and I am helped. Therefore, my heart greatly rejoices, and with my song I will praise him" (Ps. 28:6–7). "Praised be the LORD, for he has wondrously shown his goodness to me" (Ps. 31:21).

One can observe with this deliverance that it often comes very rapidly and at the most unexpected time—mostly when little time is offered before death, just as was shown in several earlier examples, also those of martyrs. "Then your light will break forth like the morning, your healing will spring forth speedily" (Isa. 58:8). "That is the voice of my beloved; look, he comes" (Song of Sol. 2:8).

Sometimes the deliverance comes slowly. Thus, it says twice in Job, "After this the Lord appeared to Job in a storm" (38:1; 40:1). Augustine asks here, "O Lord, how do you appear when you do this? What is the sign of your coming? Are tears and sighs also witnesses and forerunners of this comfort and of this joy?" Augustine wants to say with this that it is a good sign for the soul if it becomes undone and can begin to be broken and to melt away in groaning and weeping. Thus, the soul sighs and begins to see Jesus and strives and works so that (even if it cannot embrace him) it will take the fringe of his garment, and the soul clings to the least sign of his that it can find in order to go further.

The martyr Guido de Brès prayed, "Lord, do not leave me so that I will not leave you"; Anna Bourges prayed the same. David said, "My soul follows close behind you" (Ps. 63:8). The soul does not let him go, wherever it can take hold of him. Jacob said, "Until you bless me." And it says about the crowd in Luke 4:42, "They came to him and tried to keep him from leaving them." We read of the disciples of Emmaus, "They constrained him, saying, 'Stay with us, for it is nearly evening and the day is gone.' And he went in to stay with them" (Luke 24:29). Ruth said to Naomi, "Do not contradict me and say that I should leave you and turn away from you; because where you go I will go, and where you stay I will stay" (Ruth 1:16). Elisha said the same to Elijah: "As surely as the LORD lives and your soul lives, I will not leave you" (2 Kings 2:2).

It goes with the soul as with that Athenian who held the ship with a rope. When one hand was hacked off, he still held the rope with the other, and when that was hacked off, he held the rope with his teeth as long as he could. So also the soul does not let go what it has but persists until the end. "O LORD, we have waited for you in the way of your judgments. The desire of our soul is for your name and for the remembrance of you. With my soul I have desired you in the night; also, by my spirit within me I will seek you early" (Isa. 26:8–9). The bride also says, "I held him firmly and did not let him go" (Song of Sol. 3:4). When Jesus proposed that the disciples leave him, Peter said, "Lord, to whom shall we go? You have the words of eternal life" (John 6:68). And when Christ sees such diligence and steadfastness, he is completely moved to sustain the soul and to live with it. "Will God not avenge his own elect, who cry out day and night to him, though he bears long with them?" (Luke 18:7). And now their cry is, "Strengthen, O God, what you have done for us" (Ps. 68:28).

Thus, the deliverance frequently comes when it looks very dark for the soul and the abandonment is at its worst. The Jewish writer Philo says that divine help is the closest when human help seems far away. "Therefore," he says, "we must be of good courage, because God will certainly help us since Cajus the enemy rages against us so fiercely." Abraham stretched out his hand and took the knife to slaughter his son when God called, "Abraham, Abraham!" The martyr Nicolas Russeau (1557) said, "God usually helps his own when the barbaric persecutions are at their worst in order to show that such deliverance and help come only from him and from no one or nothing else."

In and with the deliverance comes, first, softening, lightening of the evil. The evil then becomes bearable and allows the person to breathe so that now he dares and may say with Isaiah, "I thank you, Lord, that you were angry with me, but now your anger is turned away, and you comfort me" (12:1).

The Lord now lifts his hand slightly and allows the soul to look upward. "Look away from me so that I may gain strength" (Ps. 39:13). It is the same with physical ailments—health usually comes first with such lightening.

Second, there comes a complete taking away of the evil that up to now so frightened and plagued the person. "You will be far from oppression, for you will not fear; and from terror, for it will not come near you" (Isa. 54:14). Also, the burden of sin that was the cause of the oppression is taken away. "I have blotted out your transgressions like a mist and your sins like a cloud. Return to me, for I have redeemed you" (Isa. 44:22). And we read in Isaiah 49:9–10, "That you may say to the prisoners, 'Go forth,' to those who are in darkness, 'Show yourselves.' They will feed along the roads, and their pastures will be on all high places. They will neither hunger nor thirst; neither heat nor sun will strike them."

Third, there comes a rest and peace in God, our Savior, contrary to the unrest and struggle that the soul had. "For the Compassionate One will lead them, and he will gently lead them by the springs of water." Psalm 116:7–8 says, "Be at rest once more, O my soul, for the Lord has been good to you. For you, O Lord, have delivered my soul from death, my eyes from tears, my feet from stumbling." And Augustine testifies, "Because you made us for yourself, our hearts will not rest until they find rest in you."

Fourth, there also is (which should here receive the most attention from us) joy in God—joy for the feeling of assurance of our salvation. Augustine says, "Who can give joy as he does, who made everything that gives joy?" Isaiah says, "Whereas you have been forsaken and hated so that no one went through you, I will make you an eternal excellence, a joy from generation to generation" (60:15). And in 51:11, he says, "With everlasting joy on their heads they will obtain joy and gladness; sorrow and sighing will flee away." See also 12:3: "Therefore with joy you will draw water from the wells of salvation." "His soul will dwell in prosperity" (Ps. 25:13). "Then our mouths were filled with laughter and our tongues with singing" (Ps. 126:2). (See also Isa. 25:9; 29:19.) Nehemiah says, "The joy of the Lord is your strength" (8:10). Just as the sadness was the greatest possible, so now also is the joy, and the salvation and comfort come from him who also made the burden even heavier. "They rejoiced, for God had made them rejoice with great joy. The women and the children also rejoiced so that the joy of Jerusalem was heard afar off" (Neh. 12:43). In Isaiah it says, "They will rejoice before you according to the joy of harvest, as men rejoice when they divide the spoil" (9:3). And David says, "You have put gladness in my heart, more than in the season when their grain and wine increased" (Ps. 4:7). And in Psalm 31:19, "Oh, how great is your goodness, which you have laid up for those who fear you." They become as if drunk with joy, with a "spiritual drunkenness." Then it is, "Friends, eat, drink, and become drunk." Pagan writers also mention continuous drunkenness as a reward for righteousness.

The soul tastes a joy more and greater than its sadness was before. "Make us glad according to the days in which you have afflicted us, the years in which we have seen evil" (Ps. 90:15). In the same way, Job was doubly blessed after his deliverance, because "the Lord turned away the captivity of Job when he prayed for his friends. Indeed, the Lord gave Job twice as much as he had before" (Job 42:10).

The Lord sends a continuous joy. "The meek also will have joy upon joy in the LORD, and the poor among men will rejoice in the Holy One of Israel" (Isa. 29:19).

Yes, he gives eternal joy. "'With everlasting kindness I will have mercy on you,' says the LORD, your Redeemer" (Isa. 54:8), and, "Whereas you have been forsaken and hated so that no one traveled through you, I will make you an eternal excellence, a joy from generation to generation" (Isa. 60:15). See also Isaiah 51:11: "Eternal joy shall be on their head."

Bernard says in *The Song of Solomon,* "Dear Jesus, you frequently delivered me from such great bitterness. How many times have you poured out the anointing of your mercy and the oil of your joy over my wounded conscience, after fearful weeping, after inexpressible sighing and gasping! How frequently the prayer that I began nearly in despair made me cheerful and trusting in grace!" Others who have been so embattled know that the Lord Jesus truly is a physician who heals broken hearts (Ps. 147) and binds their wounds. Let those who have not felt this still believe in him—he who says, "The Spirit of the Lord is on me, to bring good tidings to the meek and to bind up the brokenhearted" (Isa. 61:1; Luke 4:18). If they still doubt, let them come themselves and verify so that they themselves learn to understand what it means, "I want mercy and not sacrifice." And in a different place Bernard says:

> I cannot restrain myself from joy that this Majesty has condescended with such sweet affection, to bend himself to our weakness, and that this highest Godhead becomes, as it were, betrothed to the cheerful soul and is not abashed to show fondness to her like that of the most tender, love-inspired bridegroom. I do not doubt that it will be in heaven as I read about it on earth. The soul will certainly feel what the Word says, except the soul cannot now express how much it will receive in the hereafter, nor what it has already now. What do you think the soul will receive there, who here already tasted such affection that it feels as if embraced by God's arms, caressed in God's bosom, and feels so protected by God's care and safekeeping that in its rest it will be awakened by no one, whosoever, before it awakens of its own?

Chrysostom, in his *Homilies,* speaks in the same manner about this spiritual happiness.

Among the martyrs there are several who, especially when facing death, often enjoyed this spiritual joy as in a full flood and so testified. Thus, God is wont to give to his own, whom he calls to the heaviest persecutions and the heaviest cross, also a greater measure of heavenly joy already here. Adolf von Clarebach, a young and learned man and teacher in Wezel, was publicly burned at the stake beside Petrus Flisted in Cologne in 1529. When he came to the place of execution, he called out loudly that his heart and his body were so joyful and cheerful that he did not believe that any person in the whole world was more cheerful and peaceful than he.

Anna Askew, a noble lady in England, signed the confession of her faith in prison in 1546 in these words: "Anna Askew, who does neither wish for nor much fear death but is as cheerful of heart as a person can be who is on the way to heaven."

Peter Scriba, a student in Lausanne in the year 1557, testified, "The least comfort and joy that I now feel daily while in these chains is greater and more excellent than all former joy that I ever experienced in all my life." Peter Bergier, standing at the stake in the year 1555, ready to be burned, still exclaimed, "O Lord, how sweet and beloved is your name." Dyonysius Peloquin wrote to his wife from prison in 1553, "Concerning myself, I tell you the truth that never in my life have I been so genuinely cheerful and satisfied as I am presently, because I feel that the good God who has given me his grace and mercy will take me into his kingdom and will make an end to all my suffering and misery." In the year 1555, Franciscus Gamba, an Italian, spoke as follows: "My heart is flooded with such comfort that I find in myself such a joy as cannot be understood by human sense and understanding." Louis Pachal wrote in a letter to his former congregation, "It is with me that the closer I come to the time in which I will be sacrificed for my Lord Jesus Christ, the more I experience joy and gladness in my heart. Yes, I feel inexpressible joy in my heart, and I imagine that I am already out and free from my prison. I am also ready to die for Christ's sake, not just once but, if this were possible, a thousand times." Guido de Brès of Bergen in Henegouwen spoke thus in the year 1567: "Oh, dear brothers, how precious it is to have a clear conscience! I feel such a great joy in my heart that no words can express it."

This joy is expressed especially after heavy trials, when those who are saved speak from a vital feeling of deliverance. We will now pass by the examples that we already related; neither will we speak of those whom the Roman Catholics want to mention, such as Catherine of Sienna, Theresa, Tauler, and others, or of Mattheus Wejer (whose writings were published by John Spes in Dutch in 1579 and in High German in Frankfort in 1633). But we want to tell about the example of Pomponius Algerius, who died a martyr's death in the year 1555. He was born in Capua and studied in Padua. There he was captured at the command of the pope, taken from there to Venice and then to Rome, where he was burned at the stake. From his prison in Venice he wrote this very comforting letter to the faithful believers of the pure truth:

> In order to soften the sadness you suffer because of me, I cannot omit to tell you something of my pleasure and joy so that you may rejoice with me and praise the Lord. I will say what no person will want to believe when I tell it. I have found a nest of honey and honeycombs in the bowels of a lion. Who will believe what I say? Or what person will be able to imagine that one can find a paradise of pleasure in a deep and dark cave? That there is rest and hope of life in the place of sadness and death? That one finds joy in one's soul in a hell hole? Isn't it nearly unbelievable to be joyful in a place where other people weep? To be full of strength and full of courage where others fear and tremble! Who would be able to imagine this or dare to believe it? To enjoy such pleasure in such a miserable condition. To find a company of good people in such a lonely place. To find such rest in tight bands and cold irons. Dear brothers! The good hand of God has done all of this for me. Look, the One who once was far from me is now present; he is with me; him whom I could hardly notice I now see very clearly; him whom I once saw from afar is now close by. He after whom I once hungered comes and offers me his hand. He comforts and overwhelms me with gladness. He drives away all bitterness; he gives all strength and courage. He heals and refreshes me, makes me continue and comforts me. Oh, how good is the Lord, who does not allow his servants to be tempted above what they are able! Oh, how light and pleasant is his yoke! Is there anyone like the Almighty, who takes up the burdened, heals and refreshes the wounded? Is there anyone like him? Learn, my dearly beloved, how loving the Lord is, how good and merciful he is who visits his servants in their trials and condescends to allow them to enjoy his companionship in such terrible and stinking holes.

John Morellius in France wrote a certain letter in 1558 from his prison:

> I have learned in this struggle how terrible it is to fall into the hands of the Lord. But God is still always gracious to his own, and even though they fall, he does not permit that they be completely trampled. This he has also shown me again through his unfathomable mercy and has granted me the assurance that he has forgiven me all my horrible sins. And even though these sins were at one time red as blood to him, now they are to him whiter than snow. O sweet and lovely voice! Oh, how great is the joy of my heart because I feel that this good Father again embraces me, even though I was a lost and corrupt son. He has given me to understand that he will from now on support me with his hand, lead and direct me, and that this trial happened to me so that I would learn that it was not in my strength that I would gain the victory in this battle but that it all depends on his almighty grace and mercy.

Thus, the soul breaks out into songs of praise and glorifies the Almighty, the God of all goodness, whose gracious power the soul now finds in itself. With the poet of Psalm 126, the soul exclaims, "When the Lord brought back the imprisoned of Zion, we were like those who dreamed. Then our mouths were filled with laughter and our tongues with singing" (vv. 1–2). And with the prophet Isaiah, "In that day you will say, 'I thank you, Lord, that you were angry with me, but now your anger is turned away and you comfort me'" (12:1). See also Isaiah 44:23; 49:13; as well as 66:10, "I am very joyful in the Lord," and Psalm 30:11, "You have turned my mourning into dancing; you have loosened my sackcloth and girded me with gladness." And finally Psalm 146:1–2: "O my soul, praise the Lord! I will praise the Lord while I live."

Psalm 116:3 says, "The cords of death were around me, and the fears of hell had struck me; I found trouble and sorrow." That is how the soul expressed its earlier burden, and through this God's grace appears more clearly and the deliverance greater and is praised by the soul. The poet in Psalm 94:17–19 says, "Unless the Lord had been my help, my soul would soon have settled in silence. If I say, 'My foot slips,' your mercy, O Lord, will hold me up. In the multitude of my anxieties within me, your comforts delight my soul." Psalm 34:6 says, "This poor man called, and the Lord heard and saved him from all his troubles." Now the soul rejoices in this deliverance and says, "I will rejoice and be glad in your goodness, because you have seen my misery and known my soul in its troubles." Nehemiah tells about the dedication of the walls of Jerusalem: "That day they offered many sacrifices, and they rejoiced, for God had made them rejoice with great joy. The women and the children also rejoiced, so that the joy of Jerusalem was heard afar off" (Neh. 12:43).

So it is with the soul in trial; it does not rejoice alone, but all the pious and friends rejoice with it. "Rejoice with Jerusalem, and be glad with her, all you who love her; rejoice for joy with her, all you who mourned for her" (Isa. 66:10).

This appeal also comforts and strengthens all others, for we read, "Those who know your name will trust you because you, LORD, have not forsaken those who seek you" (Ps. 9:10). Oh, what an inexpressible and abundant joy now overflows this heart after its trials and dryness! What a heavenly feeling now comes to the heart in this living experience of God's return and the renewed embrace of its beloved Savior, which it sought with such consuming oppression and towering fear—until the heart found him! "Look! Your father and I anxiously sought you" (Luke 2:48). The heart is full, yes, it is spiritually drunk in this renewed wedding feast; there the soul eats good food and delights in the fatness.

Oh, the soul thinks of nothing except God, and whatever it says has reference to Christ! The soul needed one thing, and it has found that one. "And when the woman had found the piece of silver, she called her women friends and neighbors and said, 'Rejoice with me'" (Luke 15:9). The soul triumphs just like those who come from battle, like one who comes from Bozra with festive clothing, in adorned garments; the soul sings a song, a song to her beloved, an eternal hallelujah. Augustine says, "The crown of life is promised only to those who fight."

Dutch Reformed Translation Society

"The Heritage of the Ages for Today"
P.O. Box 7083
Grand Rapids, MI 49510

The board gratefully acknowledges the financial support of individual patrons, foundations, and academic institutions that met the costs of this translation.

Lifetime membership in the Dutch Reformed Translation Society is available for a onetime, tax-deductible gift of $100. Members support the society's continuing work, receive periodic newsletters, and may purchase society publications at the cost of production. Membership gifts may be sent to P.O. Box 7083, Grand Rapids, MI 49510.